THE MA[KING]
OF BRITAIN

The Age of
Expansion

THE MAKING OF BRITAIN

The Age of Expansion

edited by

Lesley M. Smith

A CHANNEL
FOUR BOOK

MACMILLAN

First published 1986

Published by
MACMILLAN EDUCATION LTD
Houndmills, Basingstoke, Hampshire RG21 2XS
and London
Companies and representatives
throughout the world

Typeset and designed by Columns of Reading

Printed in Great Britain by
R J Acford
Chichester Sussex

British Library Cataloguing in Publication Data
Smith, Lesley M.
The Making of Britain.— (A Channel Four book)
Vol. 3: The age of expansion
1. Great Britain — History
I. Title
941 DA30
ISBN 0–333–40601–X
ISBN 0–333–40602–8 Pbk

Contents

List of Illustrations

Acknowledgements

The publishers wish to acknowledge the following illustration sources:

The National Portrait Gallery; The British Library; The Bodleian Library; Yale Centre for British Art; The Society of Antiquaries of London; The Royal College of Arms; The National Library of Scotland; The Lord Chamberlain's Office; St Andrews University Library; Central Reference Library, Edinburgh; The National Gallery of Scotland; The National Maritime Museum; The Ashmolean Museum; E.T. Archive; National Museum of Wales; Northampton-shire County Record Office; The British Museum; Parker Gallery; The National Gallery, Prague; Centre for Population Studies; Cambridge-shire County Record Office; Royal Commission on Historical Monuments; Victoria and Albert Museum; Bridgeman Art Library; His Grace, The Duke of Atholl.

Every effort has been made to trace all the copyright holders but if any have been inadvertently overlooked the publishers will be pleased to make the necessary arrangement at the first opportunity.

Preface

Once again, this volume accompanies the London Weekend Television/Channel Four series *The Making of Britain*. I should like to thank those at London Weekend Television who have been involved in the production of the series: Jane Hewland, Julian Norridge, David Coulter and Paul Wallace. My thanks are due also to the contributors themselves. They have shared their knowledge of early modern Britain most generously, and have tolerated constant pleas for elucidation with much patience and charm. Several other scholars have also helped me with the preparation for the book and the series, and I should like to thank in particular Simon Adams, Peter Clark, Nicholas and Sarah Davidson, Michael Hunter, Professor J. R. Jones, Jennifer Loach, John Morrill, Roy Porter, Paul Slack and Blair Worden. Joanna Mitchell accomplished the picture research for the book and series with immense thoroughness, while Pam Wilkinson and Beverley Spurdens once again typed quickly and efficiently a very difficult manuscript. Vanessa Peerless and Michael Jupe of the Macmillan Press have been very patient editors. Finally, I should like to add a personal note of thanks to those who supervised my own studies on seventeenth-century Britain – Professor Anthony Upton (of the University of St Andrews), whose undergraduate courses in British history first interested me in the Civil War and Interregnum, and Lord Dacre of Glanton (now of Peterhouse College, Cambridge) who supervised my doctoral research. I hope that this book conveys the spirit of their teaching.

L.M.S.
London, May 1985

Introduction

Ever since the Romans abandoned the province of Britain in the early fifth century, historians, philosophers and even untutored kings had attempted to revive the concept of a heritage common to all people dwelling in these rather sparsely-populated islands off the north-west coast of Europe. Usually, such revivals coincided with yet another attempt by the bellicose kings of England to subjugate the troublesome Welsh, Scots or Irish. For centuries, the claim to rule all of Britain was an empty boast, part of the rhetoric by which rival kings played the ritualised chess game that passed for power politics in their day. But during the sixteenth century and, even more, the seventeenth century, a new urgency, and indeed a new reality, infused men's descriptions of the intrinsic and inviolable unity of Britain. By the middle of the eighteenth century there was not only a single king for all three nations of Britain but also one government whose policies were determined by British experiences and dictated by genuinely British needs.

Oddly enough, the first example of this new and permanent interest in British unity did not come from the military victories of a particularly successful king. It emerged instead from the ideological chaos afflicting Europe in the generations after the spiritual and intellectual hegemony of the universal church in Rome was shattered in the early sixteenth century. Whether the walls were breached by reformers so deeply concerned to preserve the church from error that they were reluctantly forced to secede from it, or by princes who cynically rode the bandwagon of conviction to seize the wealth and power of the church, the result was the same – a new world in which the church where one chose to pray was a test of loyalty to the state and the all-important factor in determining political survival. Worshipping God according to one's conscience became a perilous business. These extreme conditions produced a generation of men and women who were willing to place the ideal of religious freedom and independence from Rome above the temporarily outdated ties of patriotism and national identity.

One such man was the Scot, Anthony Gilby. He is perhaps better known as an acolyte of that redoubtable Scots reformer, John Knox, than as an apologist for British unity. Nevertheless, his experience of being forced into exile by a government in Scotland hostile to any opinion that diverged from Catholic orthodoxy drove him into reassessing the traditional nationalistic divisions in Britain. He argued that the Scots and, in deference to the English court that had given him refuge, the English as well, were destined to play a vital role in the victory of international Protestantism. However, he continued, the cause would be immeasurably strengthened if they could collaborate in peace 'by joyning the Ile togither in perfect religion, whom God hath so many waies coupled and strengthened by his work in nature'. Other Scottish exiles in England, or in the Protestant courts and cities of Europe, shared Gilbey's views. They were willing to give dominion of Britain to England as the price of securing a Protestant reformation in Scotland. But they were an isolated minority, unable to guarantee any long-term support in Scotland for English arms. Henry VIII, Edward VI and Elizabeth I faced the problem that had bedevilled their distant predecessor, Edward I. Defeating Scottish armies was easy; ruling Scotland from Westminster almost wholly impossible. Elizabeth never even made the mistake of joining battle, and wisely followed a course of half-open subvention by subsidy.

On her death, James VI, king of Scotland, inherited her throne, and united all three kingdoms. He was the first ruler to be able to claim with any degree of truth to be king of Britain, but he created no union beyond a common obeisance throughout the three nations to a single royal figure, a single throne. He had hoped to achieve more: he imagined that a constitutional union between England and Scotland would enable him to solve the problem of ruling Scotland from Westminster, but there was so little support for his ideas in either kingdom that the plan was quietly, albeit reluctantly, dropped.

Oddly enough, the imperial ambitions of the English monarchy and the apparently altruistic ambitions of the Scottish reformers were realised virtually simultaneously by a man who had little visible connection with either theory – Oliver Cromwell. As a rural, East Anglian gentleman, he had scarcely any military experience until he was approaching middle age, and only a conventional, if deeply felt, puritan attachment to religious liberty. His experience of government was confined to the administration of his local community, and it would be hard to imagine a man more unlikely to fulfil the political ambitions of courtiers, churchmen and kings. Yet he united Britain by a military conquest remarkable for both its rapidity and its thoroughness. He turned the personal union ruled by the first two Stuart monarchs into a constitutional union, summoning to sit at

Westminster the first parliament that included elected members from all three nations of Britain. He possessed the diplomatic and military skill to challenge the great powers of Europe, France, Spain and the Netherlands, and to dream of welding together a united British 'dominion' that spanned the Atlantic.

Many of Cromwell's policies were those that the Tudors and Stuarts had tried, and failed, to implement, while many of his achievements, which nowadays seem to be part and parcel of being British, were not subsequently recreated in any permanent form for more than a century. Ireland was not formally united with England and Scotland until 1801. Instead of being bound to England by conquest and dragged into all sorts of constitutional arrangements as part of England's territorial baggage, Ireland could now send members to the parliament at Westminster. It was only then that these meetings became truly representative of Britain as a whole, in geographic terms, at least. Cromwell used the army to restore order thoroughly to Britain, and kept it in being, garrisoning the country from the highlands of Scotland to the south of England, to remind parliament's subjects of their duty to pay taxes and obey the law. He did no more than Elizabeth, James and Charles hoped to do, and indeed, by the standards of the seventeenth century, particularly in Europe, he was rather more successful as an exponent of royal power than the Stuarts who both preceded and succeeded him.

Cromwell's desire to find a means of ruling Britain's American outposts from Westminster as effective as that he had devised for the three kingdoms themselves prefigured James II's plan to create a truly British commonwealth united under Westminster. Even a century later, in the 1760s, when Britain's territorial possessions stretched around the globe, neither parliament nor the prime minister possessed a coherent plan for governing such an empire.

At the restoration all these changes, like everything else associated with the republican regime, disappeared. Even when policies that had originated with Cromwell were revived, their ancestry was forgotten. The continuity in policy between Cromwell and the Stuarts was, however, important. Very different men had highly similar responses to the problems afflicting government and society in early modern Britain, and this suggests that whatever the particular and local events of any particular decade, the fundamental obstacles to stability in government were exactly the same throughout these centuries. Indeed, if one ignores the conventional boundary between the fifteenth and sixteenth centuries that traditionally divides medieval from modern history, and looks back over the preceding centuries, it is clear that the stability of England, and England alone, under the Tudors was something of a temporary aberration. The turbulence of the

seventeenth century, for so long seen as the personal responsibility of
the inept Stuarts, was far more the usual condition of government in
Britain, and the problems solved in the eighteenth century were
essentially those for the middle ages. Firstly, it was difficult to govern
a complex state with no army, bureaucracy or even hard cash;
secondly, the relation between crown and church and the rivalry over
which institution should wield greatest power in the state had never
been settled. Finally, relations between England, Scotland and Ireland
had to be rationalised so that all three nations could co-exist in peace.
Yet while the obstacles to stability in the sixteenth and seventeenth
centuries were so similar to those of the middle ages, the ways in
which the political classes thought about them were beginning to
change.

In an age when the king's powers were theoretically absolute, it was
in his actions that the fate of the kingdom lay. David Starkey shows
how the Tudor monarchs of England devised a number of short-term
solutions to the age-old problem of ruling with neither army nor
bureaucracy to support royal authority. He indicates how skilfully
they created a myth of royal authority that dissuaded all but the most
foolhardy from more than tacit disobedience in minor matters. But he
also demonstrates that tolerance and trust were essential ingredients in
this compromise.

These were qualities well appreciated by James vi of Scotland, who
became the first king to rule Britain, and to rule the entire country
from Westminster. Jenny Wormald argues that the skill he deployed in
managing men, and knowing when diplomatic retreat was more
prudent than confrontation, gave the union of the three kingdoms that
he achieved through dynastic accident such a secure base that its
integrity was never again permanently challenged. Kevin Sharpe charts
the by no means inevitable breakdown of trust when the three
kingdoms were inherited by a man who believed implicitly in the
rhetoric of royal power – Charles i. The Tudors had used their myth
of omnipotence to shield their lack of real power and resources;
Charles made it the basis of his every political decision. Unlike his
predecessors, Charles actually meant what he said, and in extending
this dynamic interpretation of the role of government to both Scotland
and Ireland he brought about his own downfall.

Neither the civil wars, nor the constitutional experiments of the
Interregnum, created for the somewhat unwieldy kingdom of Britain a
government whose political power matched its aspirations. Mark
Goldie and William Speck trace the way in which the instability this
disparity inevitably caused disappeared in a way unthinkable to the
monarchs of the early seventeenth century.

The Stuart monarchy was restored in 1660, in the person of Charles

II. He reversed the Tudors' myth to present a complaisant and compliant facade to the nation while exercising more direct power than any of his predecessors. At the same time, the king was slowly distancing himself from the arena of political in-fighting and decision-making in parliament. He did this by employing one of his most trusted servants in the position of 'prime minister' to manage parliament. In many ways, such a man was no more than the king's stalking horse, who could always be disowned if his policies proved unpopular. The sense that the king was no longer so directly involved in the minutiae of politics was accentuated by the formation of political parties, whose members fought elections across the country and sat in parliament to represent a particular viewpoint. Now the political nation began to judge its allegiance not on the old call of 'king or country' but on the much less disruptive (at least in seventeenth-century terms) cry of 'Whig' or 'Tory'. Both could claim that such party loyalties were still compatible with their first allegiance, to the house of Stuart. The relative peace attending the deposition of James II in 1688 and the coronation of William III in his place demonstrates just how low the political temperature in Britain had dropped.

This glorious revolution brought a foreigner to the throne of Britain. His priorities were quite different from those of his predecessors: he was fundamentally uninterested in Britain as anything more than a treasure chest ample enough to finance his wars against Louis XIV of France. In exchange for a strong army and adequate subsidy, he surrendered on many more contentious issues.

The strange line of succession to William, a rather gullible woman and a German prince, introduced further monarchs to the throne of Britain who were simply not interested in the old political problems. Within a remarkably short time, Britain had entered a period of stability that was all the more surprising given the revolutions that afflicted the other great powers of Europe in the eighteenth and nineteenth centuries.

To modern eyes, the fact that the ancestors of today's wholly secular political parties drew their allegiance from differing opinions on religion seems distinctly odd. But throughout the middle ages religion frequently seemed to be no more than a branch of politics in which the internationalist aspirations of theologians clashed with the nationalist views of kings and princes. Christopher Haigh explains how this clash of interests ended when a series of short-term decisions in England and Scotland led to the abandonment of the universal church in Rome because such allegiance was politically inexpedient. Once the hegemony of the church was broken, a new latitude entered the sphere of religious life. At first the competition between churches led to a rigid statement of doctrine on all sides, and a more thorough persecution of Dissenters. When the precise way in which one worshipped was no longer sanctified by the prospect of a martyr's death, religious belief became simply one facet of political and social life; a private matter to be settled by the private conscience. But by the end of the seventeenth century the very diversity of religious expression available in Britain meant that toleration was inevitable.

Contrary to popular belief, that sees this reformation in faith and the place of religion in society as the work of kings such as Henry VIII and truly exceptional men such as John Knox, the ordinary people of Britain exercised a great deal of influence over its precise course. Ronald Hutton, Keith Wrightson and Margaret Spufford all explore the history of those who lived far from the royal courts of London and Edinburgh and whose only contact with government came when they broke the law or did not pay their taxes. Yet even from this domestic compass their influence on the way Britain has developed is striking. When the two sides in the Civil War reached stalemate in 1645, the distaste of the ordinary people for the war, their reluctance to fight, or to pay for others to do so, brought the armies of the king to defeat quicker than all the military reforms of the parliamentarians.

In peacetime, the horizons of ordinary people were much narrower, but even there a more diverse way of life was emerging. People began to acquire for the first time the household and domestic goods — sheets and pillows, cutlery, plates, curtains and suits of clothes — that are so much a part of modern life. In many ways, our own preoccupation with 'getting and spending' began in the prosperity of ordinary people in the seventeenth century. One aspect of ordinary life that has remained constant is the preoccupation of individuals with their families and friends. Sixteenth-century rulers wanted to know more about the people they ruled: they ordered parishes to keep records of births, marriages and deaths; they tried to make justice more efficient by introducing record-keeping at all levels of the legal system; they drew maps and plans to show where people lived, and who owned land. This bureaucratic accumulation of detail reveals across the centuries the intimate side of life in early modern Britain; the course of a love affair, or the death of a child; the cost of a wedding, or the amount of ale drunk at a village feast. It reveals also that this world was acquiring more than a passing interest in politics and world affairs, an interest satisfied by the newsbooks, broadsheets and almanacs pouring from the new printing presses in ever-increasing numbers.

At the same time, more and more people learned to read. The language they read was English, but as Elizabeth Cook explains, it was a language undergoing far-reaching changes. As men discovered more and more about the world in which they lived, they had to find new words to describe that world, and new ways to use English to interpret it. In the hands of poets such as Shakespeare and Milton, or of philosophers such as Francis Bacon and Thomas Hobbes, the English language achieved a clarity and richness of expression that is perhaps unrivalled to the present day.

The expansion of language reflected the way in which Britain's interest in the world beyond its frontiers was growing. The wealth the Spaniards plundered from the new world (and which was plundered in turn by English pirates like Sir Francis Drake) tempted Britons into unknown waters and unknown lands. Disorganised, greedy and idealistic, the first colonists had too few resources for conquest. Instead, they turned to settlement and trade; although this course was prosaic, Bruce Lenman shows how this strategy built for Britain an empire that, by the middle of the eighteenth century, stretched around the globe. By abandoning glory for the tradesman's hat, the British government forged a policy that enabled them to build a second, and bigger, empire when the first collapsed with the American revolution.

The fact that it was Britain, and not the richer and more populous countries of Europe such as France and Spain, that developed this precocious empire is paradoxical. Louis Cullen, in the final chapter, goes some way to solving this mystery by surveying the way in which Britain developed into a single, united kingdom in the eighteenth century. This was no debilitating political take-over, but an unusually flexible union which concentrated financial resources, manpower and policy-making in the hands of the Westminster government but did not destroy the vitality of the kingdoms of Ireland and Scotland that was so essential to the imperial plans of later generations. The seemingly intractable problems of the middle ages no longer existed. Here, in the early modern world, were laid the foundations of unity, stability and trade that propelled Britain to its eventual, albeit transitory, world power.

The Reformation

Christopher Haigh

In 1563 John Foxe, an English Protestant preacher, published *The Acts and Monuments*, a highly influential work which soon became known as *The Book of Martyrs*. It was one of the first histories of the English Reformation – the sixteenth-century political and religious crisis, in which Henry VIII and his successors broke away from the international Roman Catholic Church and established a national Protestant Church of England. John Foxe's book tells a compelling story, of oppression by the corrupt medieval Catholic Church, of resistance by heroic Protestant martyrs, and of the mounting strength of a powerful Protestant movement in England. It ends with the momentous victory of Protestantism in 1559, when the great English Reformation vanquished ancient superstition and the English people enthusiastically embraced the Protestant religion – or that, at least, was how John Foxe saw it. And, partly through the influence of Foxe, that was how later generations of English men and women have seen it. The Foxe version came to dominate our understanding of a key period in our past.[1]

But Foxe wrote propaganda, not history: he wrote to condemn the Catholics and to praise the Protestants; he wrote to justify the Reformation as a great movement of spiritual liberation and national reconstruction. Now, more than four hundred years after Foxe, the perspective is rather different. In a more ecumenical age, it is no longer axiomatic that the Catholics were bad and the Protestants good; and we are no longer dependent for our knowledge of the Reformation upon writers such as Foxe. The last twenty years have seen a determined investigation of the central and local records of the political and religious history of Tudor England. As more and more research has been done, Reformation history has become very much more complicated – and very much less heroic – than John Foxe's story and English national tradition.[2]

Historians have always tried to make the past manageable by subdividing and simplifying it. We break the continuous flow of time into artificial periods for our own convenience; we isolate themes from the confusion of simultaneous happenings. We select events which seem to have something in common, lump them together, call them a 'movement' or a 'period', and then treat our own composite creation as a historical reality. We too frequently forget that 'the Renaissance', 'the Enlightenment' and 'the rise of nationalism' are no more than our own simplifying labels.

We have treated 'the Reformation' as if it was a unified movement and a single coherent event – as if King Henry VIII in 1529 could throw a switch on the control-panel of history, and unleash thirty years of inexorable change. Also we have tended to forget that the Reformation happened in different ways in the various parts of the British Isles. But 'the Reformation' was not one big event; it is just a convenient historians' label for a collection of little events. The term 'Reformation' links together a large number of separate changes in religious institutions and ideas, spread across many years – an attack on the power of priests, a rejection of the authority of the pope, a confiscation of church property, a suppression of Catholic organisations, the introduction of an English Bible and of Protestant church services, and a redefinition of prescribed beliefs. In sum, such changes would constitute a total 'Reformation'. There were committed Protestant reformers in Tudor England and Stuart Scotland who wanted such a wholesale Reformation, who wanted to follow the example of Martin Luther in Germany – but they were not the men who took the decisions. Though, as we shall see, the Reformation in Scotland was to be rather different, the English Reformation actually happened as a series of little events, as princes and politicians calculated their advantages and decided on their next moves.[3] They did not implement, stage by stage, a pre-conceived Reformation plan; they took tactical decisions based on short-term considerations. They did not know they were participating in a 'Reformation': they thought they were simply governing the kingdom as best they could.

The great figures of the political Reformation in England – Henry VIII, Thomas Cromwell, the dukes of Norfolk, Somerset and Northumberland – did not elect for or against 'the Reformation' in one do-or-die decision. They made a number of smaller choices: for or against Cardinal Wolsey in 1529, when the nobles overthrew a powerful churchman; then for or against canon law in 1532, when the king wished to seize control of the church; then for or against the Aragon divorce in 1533, when Henry VIII wanted to marry Anne Boleyn; then for or against papal power in 1534, when the pope tried to force Henry to give up his new wife; then for or against the smaller monasteries in 1536, when the government needed their wealth to pay for new fortifications on the south coast; and so on. Sometimes, the

1.1. Thomas Cromwell

1.2. Cardinal Wolsey

consensus of political opinion was that further change was advantageous: if Catholic France and the empire of Charles V were in close alliance, then political calculation dictated another step towards Protestantism, to attract allies among the Lutheran princes of Germany. But if France and the empire seemed about to divide, as in 1540, then a more conservative stance in religion might gain the support of the Catholic Holy Roman Emperor. The English Reformation did not take place in an international vacuum, and the balance of European power could never be ignored.

Neither could the balance of opinion in England be neglected. The Tudor state had, after all, no standing army and only a small central bureaucracy; it relied for its policing on the co-operation of local gentlemen, working as unpaid justices of the peace.[4] The state, therefore, could only enforce what was broadly acceptable, and it could not overcome any widespread resistance. A large dose of Reformation in the summer of 1536 provoked a huge northern rebellion in the autumn of that year, a rising known as the Pilgrimage of Grace, and, after a face-saving interval, Henry VIII had to withdraw some objectionable proposals. By 1539 the committed Protestants were in despair, as the authority of the king was used against them rather than in their favour. Though England did not return to the Roman obedience, Catholic orthodoxies were again enforced by law,

1.3. Frontispiece to the Bible in English, 1539. Henry VII hands Bibles to Cranmer and Cromwell who pass them on to a grateful people.

by the Act of Six Articles, called by Protestants 'the whip with six strings'.

However, the fortunes of politics were unpredictable, and the wheel could swing again in a reformist direction. If old Henry VIII had died in the summer of 1546, he would have left Catholic sympathisers such as Bishop Gardiner and the duke of Norfolk in the ascendant; the government of the boy King Edward would have been in the hands of conservatives. But Henry actually died in January 1547, and by then the conservatives had been disgraced. Control of the kingdom passed to a reformist regency council, and religious change was resumed.[5] Partly to fight off the claims of their political enemies, and partly to justify the continued spoliation of the church, Edward's ministers carried Reformation further than Henry VIII had ever wished, or ever dared.

So the Reformation did not proceed in a straightforward sequence: it tacked and turned as political interests dictated — and sometimes it went into reverse and change was undone. When Edward died in July 1553, the designated successor was the Catholic Princess Mary and the power of the Protestants was at risk. The duke of Northumberland and his allies therefore sought to change the succession, to by-pass

1.4. Edward VI

1.5. Mary Tudor

Mary in favour of the Protestant Lady Jane Grey. Their scheme was defeated by rebellion in the provinces: while many Protestants were undecided, Catholic gentry and peasants took firm action for the Catholic claimant to the throne. Queen Mary swept into power on a wave of conservative enthusiasm.[6] Mary's Catholic government soon alienated some of its support and it made a number of mistakes. It achieved notoriety in English history by burning almost three hundred Protestants at the stake. Still, the steps Mary took to unravel the Reformation were widely welcomed, and it seemed that state Catholicism was safe once more. However, Mary died in 1558, while England was officially at war with the pope and before the counter-Reformation had been made irreversible. This chance made it possible for the new Queen Elizabeth to return to the policies of her brother Edward; the Reformation resumed.

Elizabeth was hailed by her Protestant subjects as a Reformation heroine, as the English Deborah ('the judge and restorer of Israel') who would complete God's work. But Elizabeth was, for all her mild reformism, a political realist, and she made the adjustments which convenience dictated. The Prayer Book of 1559, the Uniformity Act which enforced it, and the Royal Injunctions issued by the queen, made significant concessions to conservative sensibilities.[7] Elizabeth vetoed later attempts to stiffen anti-Catholic laws and, except in periods of political crisis, the persecution of Catholics was cautious. The queen's own devotion to the Protestant cause was less than complete: in 1562 and 1579 she toyed with amendments to the religion of the state, in pursuit of marriage and her own emotional needs.[8] Only the balance of politics in 1559 made the 'Elizabethan settlement' a mainly Protestant one; only the balance of advantage thereafter made the decision of 1559 a lasting 'settlement'.

The English Reformation happened not as an inexorable sequence, but as the culmination of a succession of contingent events – of accidents which, in total, tended towards Protestant victory. To the reformist preachers, and to John Foxe, the fact that these accidents amounted to a 'Reformation' showed the hand of God in human affairs – it displayed Providence in action. Whether this was so is a matter for theologians, not for historians. But a historian can say that the piecemeal character of the English Reformation was the key to its success. To the conservative people of England, a wholesale 'Reformation' was distasteful. However, the dish was easier to swallow when some of it was fed in tasty morsels, for few laymen would oppose higher taxes paid by priests, or the nationalisation of church wealth to finance higher defence spending. The English ate their Reformation as a recalcitrant child is fed its meals, little by little, in well-timed spoonsful – 'one for Cardinal Wolsey, one for Queen Catherine, one for the Pope, one for the monks ...' – until the plate has been emptied, and Mother Providence has triumphed.

Only the prescient and the pious, a Thomas More or a John Fisher, went to the executioner's block in defence of the authority of the pope or the marriage of Catherine of Aragon. Even Catholic bishops did not recognise the significance of what was happening around them, until it was too late. 'Oh, that I had holden still with my brother Fisher, and not left him when time was', wailed Bishop Stokesley of London on his deathbed in 1539.[9] If the conservatives had known that Henry's break with Rome was not going to be just a tactical maneouvre to gain the king his divorce, then perhaps others would have stood with Fisher in 1535, but they did not know, and they could not know. For to accuse them of lack of foresight is to succumb to the false scenario of inevitable Reformation. They did not recognise that the break would be final, because it was not necessarily going to be final: Thomas Cromwell wanted it to be final, and Henry VIII was willing for it to be final, but it was only the chance of politics which would make it final.

Thus, the English Reformation was a sequence of accidents and instalments, which took the nation from official Catholicism to nominal Protestantism by a series of small steps. The Reformation happened fairly peacefully because few recognised what it was. Only in 1559, when the new Elizabethan regime tried to impose a total Reformation, was the real significance of events clear even at Westminster, and because it was now clear, the Uniformity Bill passed the House of Lords by only a slender majority.[10] It took ten years and more to implement the legislation of 1559 in many parishes, so the 'Elizabethan settlement' too slipped in little by little. Away from London and the big towns, it was not until the 1570s that the English really had to face the fact that, like it or not, they had had a Reformation![11]

Some, of course, liked what they had had. For the literate and the articulate, Protestantism was a liberating creed, which helped them cast off the thraldom of the priests. It purified the church services which some had thought insultingly superstitious, and it gave the Bible in English to those who wished to intensify their personal faith. But for the 70 per cent of men and the 90 per cent of women who could not read, the official Reformation under Henry VIII and his son had little to offer.[12] Indeed, it came to them primarily as a destructive force. It suppressed the monasteries, which had provided charity for the poor, and left their decaying buildings as reminders of what once they had been. It abolished festivals and processions, which had brought gaiety to village life; it forbade bequests to provide prayers for the dead, whose souls might now be left to languish in purgatory;

it removed the saints and their images, to which the simple had turned to pray for aid. Above all, it took away the Latin mass, the familiar celebration which had been a wonder-working spell to ward off evil.

These changes came piecemeal, and many of them were implemented slowly and sullenly. Yet their impact on the villages of England was profound, and it can be traced step by step through contemporary churchwardens' accounts, which show the churches gradually stripped bare. Candlesticks, statues, altars and crucifixes were taken down; vestments, chalices and church bells were confiscated; and one by one the old ceremonies and celebrations stopped. Such measures were spread over some years, but together they undermined the simple religion of ordinary people and brought, in its place, a creed which seemed suited only for those abused as 'scripture men' and 'precise fools'.[13]

In England and Wales, political circumstance had brought a slow Reformation, which happened almost imperceptibly and without revolution. In Scotland, it was very different. Protestantism spread there in the 1530s and after, especially among the lairds of the lowlands, many of whom looked to England for advancement. But during the long minority of Mary, Queen of Scots, the influence of the French kept the Scottish state hostile to the Reformation. In 1559–60, fired by the preaching of John Knox and by the prospect of church property, the Protestant lords led an anti-Catholic and anti-French revolution. With support from England, the Lords of the Congregation drove out Rome and France together, and in 1567 they drove out their Catholic queen Mary, and set up her child, James VI, as a puppet king in her place.[14] The Reformation in Scotland was a revolution, and not, as in England, an evolution. But on both sides of the border, the Reformation was made by interest groups and militant minorities, who used the power of the state to impose their wills upon reluctant majorities. In Ireland and Wales, the Reformation was imposed by foreigners – the interfering English – with very little support from the natives.

During the long reigns of Elizabeth of England and James of Scotland, however, Protestantism expanded and became much more popular. The universities were increasingly staffed by Calvinist tutors, who taught Genevan Protestantism to their students: they turned out new generations of Protestant ministers and magistrates. Godly preachers were successful in the ports and market towns, especially among merchants and artisans. In some country parishes, where a Protestant landlord threw his influence behind the preachers, godly communities were created.[15] On Sundays late in Elizabeth's reign, John Bruen, squire of Bruen Stapleford in Cheshire, led his family, servants and tenants along the mile to Tarvin parish church; they sang psalms on their way, went to morning service, discussed the sermon as they picnicked outside the church, heard the afternoon sermon, and then returned home, again singing psalms as they went.[16]

However, the efforts of squire and parson were not uniformly successful in England or Scotland, and were hardly successful at all in Ireland and in Wales. John Bruen brought in preachers to Tarvin, but they were 'much slighted by many, little regarded by the vulgar sort, much opposed by the popish and profane, and too much undervalued by all'.[17] Parishioners did not sit in attentive rows, listening to sermons Sunday by Sunday; they chattered and scoffed, and if they grew bored they slept or walked out. Though Protestantism became a more popular religion in the reign of Elizabeth I, it remained a minority religion, and many aspects of it were bitterly resented.

The Calvinist doctrine of predestination and the stress upon Bible reading seemed to restrict salvation to the respectable and the educated. The preachers' attacks upon old village customs, such as religious plays and festival banquets, made their religion seem joyless. Their insistence upon strict observance of the Sabbath, which led to the closure of alehouses and the prohibition of Sunday dancing, angered those who were losing their one day of relaxation. Furthermore, when ministers restricted their hospitality and their visiting to the known godly (while of course claiming tithes from the rest), they seemed to confirm that they cared nothing for the needs of the majority. By the 1580s, many towns and villages were deeply divided between the godly Protestants, led by the ministers, and the rest of the parishioners, often led by alehouse-keepers, whose trade was threatened by the preachers' demands for Sunday closing.[18]

As the parish churches and clergy became more definitively Protestant, so the Church of England and the Church of Scotland lost many of their attractions for ordinary people. In England, some turned instead to the ministrations of 'recusant priests', old Catholic clergy who had resigned from the official church after the Elizabethan settlement. A separated Catholic Church emerged, in opposition to the established Church of England; and as the old recusant clergy died out, they were replaced by young Englishmen trained as priests in seminaries on the continent. However, the Catholic community was to be an extremely small one. This was partly because even discontented conservatives were reluctant to abandon the parish churches, which were centres of village life. It was also because of the pressures of intermittent persecution: one hundred and eighty English Catholics were executed for their religion in the reign of Elizabeth I. But, above all, it was the nature of the mission from the continental seminaries which really sealed the fate of English and Scottish Catholicism. The young missionaries, for understandable social and logistical reasons,

1.6. Preaching, from a sixteenth-century broadsheet

concentrated their attentions on the households of the gentry in the south-east of England and of the nobles in the lowlands of Scotland. Many of them became domestic chaplains to great families. The conservative peasantry, especially in the north and west of England, were neglected; they were left to go, if not quite to the devil, at least to the Church of England.[19]

Thus the missionary priests ministered mainly to the Catholic gentry, and the Calvinist clergy of the established churches ministered mainly to the Bible-reading godly. For the vast majority of the people, those who dutifully attended their parish churches but were unmoved by evangelical Protestantism, there was little provision – except, perhaps, in the dwindling number of parishes which had 'dumb-dog' ministers, whose failure to preach was more than compensated for by their willingness to chat on the ale-bench after services. The medieval Catholic Church had provided magical ceremonies which protected the people from disaster, their flocks and herds from disease and their crops from failure. But the Calvinist ministers regarded such provisions as grotesque superstitions, and preached instead a reliance on the providence of God. Therefore what the church would no longer provide, the people sought from private enterprise; they turned for remedies to village cunning-men and witches, whose prominence in the late sixteenth century is a sure sign of the failure of the clergy to meet the needs of their parishioners.[20]

The Reformation had, initially, alienated the majority of the peoples of our islands from the established churches. However, in the Church of England at least, parishioners had a weapon with which they could fight back: the Book of Common Prayer. In 1559, Queen Elizabeth had been unable to get a thoroughly Protestant service book accepted by Parliament, and she had been forced to make concessions to the Catholics. These concessions, in ceremonies, vestments, and the layout of churches, were seized upon by villagers and imposed upon their reluctant clergy. The people of Flixton in Suffolk took prayer books to church to check that their vicar was saying the services accurately, and they got him dismissed in 1590 for his nonconformity.[21] There was a long struggle at Preston Capes in Northamptonshire, between parishioners who wished to receive communion kneeling, as the prayer book decreed, and a minister who would give it only to those who sat or stood, like good Protestants; again, the people won and the minister was removed in 1604.[22] There was a popular demand for ritual: though a minority – abused as 'puritans' at the time – thought all ceremony was superstition, the rest wanted to bow and kneel and sing as the prayer book gave them leave. When in 1605 the vicar of Kirkham in Lancashire refused to use the sign of the cross in baptism, sixty-one couples took their children off to be christened elsewhere,[23] for how could a sacrament be effective if the ceremony was incomplete?

The Church of England, which had emerged from the Reformation in a distinctively Calvinist garb, was beginning to be 'Anglican'. Partly in response to the popular demand for ceremonial, and partly because of new theological justifications of the role of ritual, the late-Elizabethan bishops sought to enforce more elaborate liturgy. The state church began to be a broad church, with varieties of theology and ceremony, and it began to be a national church, which served the whole community. Above all, it became a responsive church, moulded not by Protestant theologians from Geneva or Wittenburg, or even from Canterbury and Oxford, but by the pastoral preferences of its parishioners. The consumers, the men and women in the pews, began to determine the ecclesiastical product offered to them.

The Reformation was a formative event in the making of Britain, and the Protestant reformers contributed to the development and the diversity of the peoples of our islands. The Reformation helped to make England, Ireland, Scotland and Wales different. In Tudor Ireland, Protestantism was defeated; in Wales, it was, for the time being, ignored; in Scotland, Protestantism began to influence the character of the nation. But in England it was anglicised, tamed and made English: the Reformation had not changed the English people; it was the English people who changed the Reformation.

Further reading

A.G. Dickens, *The English Reformation* (London, 1964); G.R. Elton, *Reform and Reformation* (London, 1977); C. Haigh (ed.), *The Reign of Elizabeth I* (Basingstoke, 1984); J.J. Scarisbrick, *The Reformation and the English People* (Oxford, 1984); K. Thomas, *Religion and the Decline of Magic* (London, 1971).

CHAPTER TWO

The Governance of Tudor England

David Starkey

Government is a mystery. Why many people should obey one or a few can never be taken for granted. The fact is obvious now, and there has been a stream of articles on the theme 'is Britain ungovernable?'. But in earlier times, we feel, things were a lot simpler: the machinery of government was smaller and kings were kings indeed. It is a nice thought, but like most other notions of the simple life of our ancestors, it is a myth. Their life – and government – were different from ours; they were no less problematic, however.

Not even under the Tudors, when Sir Thomas Smith, Queen Elizabeth's secretary of state, could conclude his discussion of the constitutional powers of the monarch with this ringing declaration:

> To be short, the prince is the life, the head, and the authority of all things that be done in the realm of England. And to no prince is done more honour and reverence than to the king and queen of England: no man speaketh to the prince nor serveth at the table but in adoration and kneeling.[1]

'Adoration and kneeling': it is a treatment we reserve for God. And like the heavenly god this earthly god was worshipped in his absence. The second of the royal apartments, the Presence Chamber, which contained the royal throne, was a Holy of Holies, and the throne itself an Ark of the Covenant, before which all stood bareheaded even when it was empty.

But of course the throne of sixteenth-century England was not empty. Instead it was filled with some of the most powerful personalities ever to have ruled the country. The Tudor dynasty was founded by Henry VII who contrived to combine majesty with meanness. Meanly he checked every penny of the royal accounts;

while ruthlessly he treated the nobility as no king had dared to do since King John. Henry VIII, Henry VII's son and heir, also presents a double image: in youth the handsome, athletic giant; in old age, the bloated, crotchety tyrant. Linking the two is the consistent force of his personality. He might have shirked the dull routine of government, but no king has given monarchy a more awe-inspiring public face. This grand facade of power carried him through six marriages, two great ministers, and the cataclysm of the Reformation. It enabled him, above all, to hand the throne over, unchallenged, to his nine-year-old son, Edward VI. Edward was succeeded in turn by Henry's two daughters, Mary and Elizabeth, the last of her house. There are myriad portraits of Elizabeth: the dress is always different; the long, white oval of the face is changeless. And *semper eadem*, 'always the same', was her motto. The pressures for change – in religion, in politics, in foreign policy – were enormous. But successfully, and often virtually alone against even her chosen councillors, she resisted.

To talk of the emperor's clothes in the same breath as Queen Elizabeth – she of a thousand dresses – risks absurdity. Yet her government, and that of her dynasty, was, like the emperor's new clothes, a con. When the fallen favourite, the earl of Essex, burst into

2.1. Henry VIII and his family

2.2. The coronation procession of Edward VI

the queen's bedchamber at the end of Elizabeth's reign, he was confronted only by a handful of frightened ladies and one old, grey woman: Elizabeth herself, unpainted, unwigged, undressed. And when, more soberly, the commissioners drawing up the inventory of royal property after Henry VIII's death penetrated even beyond the bedchamber into the king's 'secret study', they found it contained two chests 'with ninety-six bags, pouches and purses . . . whereof the most are very mean'; while in another 'little study' was a box without its lid 'having therein books and papers of small value'.[2] At the heart of government was not an Aladdin's cave, but a lumber room.

That the foundations of Tudor power were so shallow was one of the best kept secrets of a very secretive government. Historians have not yet fully uncovered the mystery, but some things at least are clear. Clearest is the gap between the responsibilities of government and the resources, in men and material, available to discharge them. The two main tasks of a medieval king were symbolised in the images on either side of the great seal. On the front the king sat in majesty as judge; on the back he rode in armour as the warrior-defender of his people. To these inherited duties of administering justice and maintaining public order at home and waging war abroad the Tudors added other functions. With the Reformation the monarchy took over the enforcement of religious conformity; while the worsening condition of the poor forced the government, willy-nilly, to make some sort of provision for social welfare. In both of these areas the government cajoled and regulated, but it shuffled most of the work off onto others.[3]

By modern standards the responsibilities of Tudor government were narrow, but the resources were narrower still. The king was war-lord

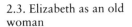

2.3. Elizabeth as an old woman

and guardian of public order yet he had neither standing army nor police force. There were, it is true, permanent garrisons at Berwick-on-Tweed, the Tower and Calais (until its loss in 1558) and a royal guard of about a hundred. But as the guard was often geriatric and the garrisons always small, it was little enough. The weakness of its military establishment left the government dangerously exposed to emergencies; more important, though, in terms of everyday govern-

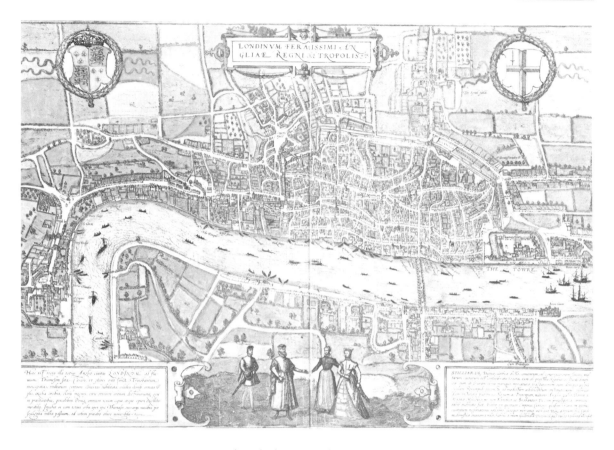

2.4. London in the sixteenth century, with the City of Westminster on the left

ment, was the slightness of the central administrative machine itself.

This was based in the former royal palace of Westminster. The king had long since abandoned the Old Palace, lying nearest the abbey, and the Tudors gave up the New Palace as well after a disastrous fire at the beginning of Henry VIII's reign. Into their place moved their civil servants. The result was rather like the requisitioning of a country house in wartime: prefabs went up in the grounds and partitions in the state apartments. The name 'Star Chamber' still conjures up nameless and largely unhistorical dread. It was housed, however, in a quaintly cottagey building on the east, or river side of New Palace Yard. At right-angles, and no more imposing, was the Exchequer; while on the other side of Westminster Hall the Court of Augmentations was built in 1537. The total cost of the basic structure was £662, or only two pounds more than Henry had spent in putting up a couple of gaily-painted canvas arches and a pavilion to entertain the French embassy of May 1527. Yet from this building costing the same as a day's revelry at court was administered all the vast wealth of the dissolved monasteries. Inside Westminster Hall itself things were still more rough-and-ready. Here in its vast spaces all three principal law

courts sat simultaneously, like classes in a dame's school. At the south end were King's Bench and Common Pleas; at the north was Chancery. All three were housed within temporary wooden partitions that could easily be dismantled when the whole hall was needed for a coronation banquet or a state trial.[4]

2.5. Design for pavilions for a tournament

Brick houses and timber partitions are a far cry from the Italianate palazzi of Victorian Whitehall or the inhuman slabs of post-war government building. They are different because the scale of government was different. The Elizabethan Exchequer was much bigger than it had been in the earlier sixteenth century: it had swallowed up the Court of Augmentations and become once more the dominant fiscal agency, handling over 90 per cent of government revenue. Yet it employed only about one hundred and fifty people, of whom half were on the government payroll.[5] Or, to put it another way, in late twentieth-century England, after Thatcher cuts and all, one person in seventy-five is a civil servant; in Tudor England the figure was probably about one in seven thousand five hundred.

Which forces us to ask how government worked at all. For part of the answer we need only go a few score yards downstream from the half burnt-out, half squatted-in semi-ruin of Westminster to Henry VIII's spanking new palace of Whitehall, which he had seized from Wolsey in 1529 and then rebuilt at breakneck speed. Here at last is scale, and cost, and numbers. The palace buildings were scattered over an irregular area some six hundred feet long and six hundred feet wide; while the main axis of the palace, the privy gallery, was about three hundred feet in length. On the building works alone Henry spent £43,000, on top of the thousands that Wolsey had already laid out. And the staff was commensurate, numbering at least five hundred and probably well over a thousand. Nor was Whitehall alone. By the end of his reign Henry had fifty-five palaces, ranging from rather run-down hunting lodges to Hampton Court and Nonsuch. Nonsuch, small but exquisite, cost £23,000; while on Hampton Court, which dwarfed even Whitehall in size and magnificence, the king had lavished a gigantic £62,000.[6]

Here manifestly, in whichever of his palaces the king and his court happened to be staying, was the centre of government. It was so politically; it was so administratively as well. The servants of the inner chambers of the palace retained, like the king himself, an important residual role in finance and the secretariat. Indeed, from the later fifteenth century to at least the end of Henry VIII's reign, it was they who looked after the all-important cash reserves. These the king kept, if not exactly under the bed, then certainly behind his bedchamber – which is why all those mean and well-used bags and purses were discovered in Henry VIII's 'secret study' after his death.[7]

The role of the king's household servants in local government was greater still. Local government was scarcely at all the concern of those professional clerks at Westminster. Instead it was self-government by the notables of the various localities. In each county, the sheriff and the justices of the peace were drawn from the most substantial knights and gentlemen of the shire. They were appointed by the king; acted in his name and received endless instructions from him. What they did not receive, however, was pay or any form of professional assistance. Instead they served at their own expense, partly as a matter of honour and partly out of self-interest.

It was a form of government that was cheap and effective. The other side of the coin was that it could pose a major problem of management. Most of the time the king could rely on the habit of obedience, reinforced by the use of the stick on the recalcitrant and the carrot on the worthy. But to know whom to punish and whom to reward far from Westminster and far even from the path of his most distant summer progresses, the king needed information, and always he required trusties on the spot. Both information and special agents were supplied, to a large extent, by the servants of the royal household.[8]

The word servant is a problem. To us it means 'lower class', but then it had no such necessary implication. The king's servants spanned the whole range from almost the bottom of the social scale to the very top. Typical of the upper reaches was Sir Thomas More, who described himself, in his own epitaph, as 'the king's good servant, but God's first'. It was as a royal servant that he was shown in Holbein's famous portrait of 1527. Traditionally his massive gold chain is seen as the emblem of the chancellorship but in fact it is simply the livery chain of a king's knight. Its most important elements are the three royal badges, or symbols of service. The chain is closed by two portcullises, the badge of Henry VIII's grandmother, Lady Margaret Beaufort, which the king adopted as his own; while from the portcullises hangs the Tudor rose itself.[9] These badges were worn in some form by all the king's servants: humble men, like yeomen of the guard, had them embroidered on their jackets; while the very greatest in the land, the twenty-six knights of the garter, the 'confreres and companions' of the sovereign, carried them in the collars of the order, which had been redesigned by Henry VIII to include the Tudor rose.[10] The royal badges were not only worn, they also appeared everywhere in the structure and furnishings of the palace itself: in the glass, the hangings, the carving, even in the covers of books.

In short the world of the early Tudor court was extraordinarily monothematic: everything and everybody exhibited the same badges. But the king's servants did not spend all their time in this world. Since they also, all but the humblest, had houses and households of their own. Most famous of these is Sir Thomas More's house at Chelsea, where he lived with his family and his own servants. Though he was a servant at court, at home, of course, he was the master. More was a Londoner-born and a lawyer, which is why he chose to live in what was then the pleasant suburban village of Chelsea. But most of the king's leading servants were, or became, gentlemen, with their houses, estates and roots firmly in the countryside.

Typical of such men was Sir Richard Clement. He had begun his career as one of Henry VII's most intimate personal attendants; had married, with the help of a royal loan, a rich widow; and had eventually used her money to buy an estate at Ightham Mote, near Sevenoaks in Kent. There was already a substantial moated manor house there, but Clement embarked on an ambitious scheme of rebuilding. He glazed windows, refronted the private apartments and built an entirely new chapel. And in everything he did he put those badges: the rose, of Tudor, of York, of Lancaster, and the portcullis, as well as the badges – the arrows, the castle, the pomegranate – of his mistress, Catherine of Aragon, Henry VIII's first queen. The result was to turn his house into a visual extension of the king's court, just as he, wearing his chain as a royal knight, was visibly the king's servant, and his representative. Together house and owner formed an outpost of royal government: Clement, a power-broker; his house, a power-house. From there master and servants would sally forth over the moat to quell a riot, help suppress a major rebellion, or even join in the king's wars abroad.[11]

Men like Clement, the wearers of the royal chain, were themselves key links in the chain that bound the king's government to the localities. Clement was a total outsider in Kent. Yet, when in 1528 the 'yeomen of Kent' were up in arms against the king's habit of demanding loans and neglecting to pay them back, Clement was one of a handful who negotiated a settlement with them.[12] This meant that in counties where there were not many Clements around the king had a problem. One such county was Northamptonshire, where in 1532 Sir William Spencer died. Spencer had grown rich on sheep-farming (though the family has recently gone on to higher things) and he had made a determined attempt to avoid the payment of feudal incidence, or death duties. The difficulty in dealing with this, it was explained to the king's minister, Thomas Cromwell, was that 'the king has so few friends in Warwickshire or Northamptonshire'. The first step was to bring in a king's servant, David Cecil, grandfather of Elizabeth's minister, from just over the border in Lincolnshire and make him sheriff. As such he would impanel the jury that would decide whether or not the king had title to Spencer's lands. In consultation with another local gentleman high in favour at court, Cecil resolved to select a jury that was 'indifferent or favourable to the king', and included among its members two of 'the king's servants, honest men'. Both of them had already been reminded that 'they may do the king service and purchase his favour', but Cromwell was advised to back the reminder up with a personal letter. This, of course, is jury nobbling, with the king as nobbler.[13]

Jury nobbling works best in small, face-to-face communities, which is what the government of Tudor England was. The king knew his servants and the servants knew their localities. Under Edward IV, Henry VIII's grandfather, a well-placed observer put it all very clearly. The king, he noted, had such a good memory that he knew 'the names and estates' of everybody who mattered, 'even, if in the district in which they lived, they held the rank only of a private gentleman'. And – because even if he knew everybody he could not know everything – Edward, he went on, 'had taken care to distribute the most trustworthy of his servants throughout all parts of the kingdom', so that 'no attempt whatever could be made in any part of the kingdom by any person . . . but what he was immediately charged with the same to his face'.[14] Sir John Fortescue, writing in the previous generation, asserted that 'the might of the land, after the might of the great lords thereof, standeth most in the king's officers and servants'.[15] Both Edward IV, and still more the Tudors after him, knew how to turn that might to their own advantage.

Or rather the earlier Tudors did. The Tudors reigned for one hundred and twenty years and that is a long time in politics, then as now. The later Tudor government is recognisably different. Two parallel incidents will make the difference plain. The most serious threat to a personal monarchy is a challenge either to the holder of the crown or to his successor. The Tudors, like every other dynasty, faced several such challenges. However, it is those that occurred in 1519–20 and in 1585 that concern us. In 1519 Henry VIII was fearful of a noble conspiracy, led by the disaffected duke of Buckingham; in 1585 Elizabeth's advisers were terrified of the web of plot and counter-plot that wove round Mary, Queen of Scots, who was at once Elizabeth's prisoner, possible successor and would-be supplanter. In such situations all governments try to drum up support. The interesting thing is how differently Elizabeth's and Henry VIII's went about it. In 1519 a 'privy remembrance', which we can translate as a top-secret memorandum, recommended

> that the king's grace do devise to put himself in strength with his most trusty servants in every shire for the surety of his royal person and succession and resisting all manner bandings.[16]

It was all very hush-hush. In 1585, on the other hand, the government sought maximum publicity. It announced that 'the life of our gracious sovereign lady Queen Elizabeth hath been most traitorously and devilshly sort', and might even have been taken 'if almighty God, her perpetual defender, of his mercy hath not revealed and withstood the same'. Then, on the principle presumably that God continues to help them who help themselves, it invited 'noblemen and other, principal gentlemen and officers . . . and justices of the peace in sundry counties' to join in subscribing to the 'Bond of Association', by which they swore to protect Elizabeth and to pursue to the death any who might assassinate her.[17]

Why this change? Let us look again at servants and the sort of incident that had provoked Henry VIII's panic of 1519. In November of that year one of Henry's servants, Sir William Bulmer, had renounced the king's service and become servant instead to the duke of Buckingham. Then, to add insult to injury, he had had the nerve to show himself at court. The king confronted him and thundered as the knight knelt cowering at his feet:

> he would none of his servants should hang on another man's sleeve, and that he was as well able to maintain him as the duke of Buckingham. And that what might be thought by his departing, and what might be supposed by the duke's retaining, he would not then declare.[18]

Note those words 'retain' and 'maintain'. They are the key terms of what historians call bastard feudalism. That is the system, prevalent in the fifteenth century, by which a lord or great gentleman 'maintained' a number of 'retainers', who wore his badge, ran his house and estates, and fought for him in battle as well. Once it used to be thought that the first Tudor, Henry VII, had wiped out bastard feudalism. Now it is clear that it is a different story. Instead of destroying bastard feudalism he sought to monopolise it; instead of suppressing badges he used them more lavishly than ever before; and instead of stamping out retaining he retained more than anyone else. In short, he sought with much success to make himself the biggest bastard feudal lord of all, with the largest following of badge-wearing retainers. And that, no more no less, is what all those royal servants, from Sir Richard Clement to Sir Thomas More, were: royal retainers.[19]

Even by 1519 the Tudors' ambition to monopolise retaining was not fully achieved, as the Bulmer incident proves. Two years later, however, the principal offender, the duke of Buckingham, was executed, and by accident and design, every other rival noble house went the same way over the next thirty years. Hence the contrast between the 'privy remembrance' and the 'Bond of Association'. In 1519 the 'king's men' are seen as the narrow group, party even, of the royal servants; by 1585 the whole ruling class was thought of in the same way: *everybody* was now – in a much looser sense of course – the queen's servant. And the symbols undergo the same transformation as the servants. In Henry VIII's reign only sworn royal servants such as Clement decorated their houses with royal badges; by Elizabeth's reign, every gentleman put the queen's arms up above his fireplace, and by the end of the century, the Tudor rose had ceased to be the badge of a house and had become the English rose, the emblem of the nation.

The rose was also Elizabeth, the virgin queen, for not only had the nature of service and therefore local government changed; so too had monarchy and central government itself. Some historians even talk of a 'revolutionary' change from medieval 'household' government to modern 'bureaucratic' government.[20] In view of what we have discovered about the inhabitants of the old palace of Westminster, that does not seem very likely. The real reason for change, I suspect, was much simpler and lay in the extraordinary accident of the late Tudor succession, which brought first a boy and then two women to the throne. Children and women, and women with female servants, could not rule as kings. The difference shows strikingly in the royal image itself: Henry VIII's portraits emphasise the huge, fleshly presence of the man; Elizabeth's on the other hand are etherealised, iconic. The person is turning into the symbol.

Elizabeth, of course, never turned into a cypher, but nor did she

2.6. The Court of
Wards, 1585, with
William Cecil presiding.

ever govern directly. Instead most everyday business was dealt with by
the high-powered committee known as the Privy Council. The result
of these changes at both centre and periphery was a markedly
different flavour all round. Rather than a king knowing people and
places personally, like Edward IV or Henry VIII, we find a great
minister, such as William Cecil, knowing about them by lists, and
registers and maps. It was not bureaucratic; but neither was it
personal.[21]

Historians, seduced by the quantity of archives the new order
created, have tended to see the change as unqualified gain for the
crown. That is too simple. For in place of the direct personal bond of
master and servant came two other ideas, both abstract. You no
longer just served the queen, but the queen as the embodiment of the
state and the Protestant religion. Nor did you any longer just serve,
you served for cash, with that ruthlessly commercial attitude to place
that Edmund Spenser satirised in the person of the Fox in *Mother
Hubbard's Tale* who appeared

> Now like a merchant . . .
> Now like a lawyer . . .
> Then would he be a broker . . .
> Then would he seem a farmer.[22]

The two attitudes are sharply contradictory, though often they co-existed in the same person: as for example, Lord Burghley, who got away with it, and Francis Bacon, who did not. Yet both attitudes presented dangers to the crown. Obviously so, with the steadily advancing tide of corruption which created resentment from those who did not benefit and even from those who did not benefit as much as others.[23] But, ironically, the greater potential danger came from the elevated notion of state service. So long as there was a monarch such as Elizabeth, whose personality made her the fitting embodiment of the state and whose policies did not challenge too strongly the dominant interest groups within it, all was well. But once those conditions ceased to be fulfilled, as they soon did under the Stuarts, the veil that concealed the mystery, and the weakness, of royal government risked being torn off completely.

Further reading

G.R. Elton, *Reform and Reformation* (London, 1977); *The Reign of Elizabeth I*, ed. Christopher Haigh (London, 1984); *The Mid-Tudor Polity*, ed. Jennifer Loach and Robert Tittler (London, 1980); J.J. Scarisbrick, *Henry VIII (London, 1968)*; R.L. Storey, *The Reign of Henry VII (London, 1968)*; Penry Williams, *The Tudor Regime* (Oxford, 1979).

The First King of Britain

Jenny Wormald

James VI and I built magnificent funerary monuments to the last sovereigns of the separate kingdoms of England and Scotland, Elizabeth and Mary. No one bothered to built a monument to the first king of Britain. The memorials to his reputation have been equally dismissive. That brilliant summary of English historical attitudes, *1066 And All That*, characterised him as the king who 'slobbered at the mouth and had favourites; he was thus a Bad King'.[1] In what is called the Whig interpretation of history – the belief in the inexorable progress of the English state towards a mixed and democratic constitution – he is the first of the great Stuart villains; for his passionate commitment to the divine right of kings, the theory that kings were answerable only to God, brought him into direct conflict with those freeborn Englishmen who made up the House of Commons, and stood for the inalienable liberties and rights of the subject. His reign ushered in the period when that conflict was most bitterly fought out, and finally resolved; it was the seventeenth century, the Stuart century, which saw the ultimate victory of constitutionalism over the royal absolutism introduced into England by a foreign monarch, James VI and I.[2] The aura of inevitability which surrounds that victory – surely freeborn Englishmen, with their traditions going back to Magna Carta were bound to triumph – surrounds something else, the union of the crowns itself. For that too had an inevitable rightness. England had been trying to rationalise the British Isles since the middle ages, by taking over Wales, Ireland and Scotland; only Scotland had successfully resisted, but now she too became part of the English hegemony. It looks straightforward enough; and if the history of the union of the crowns is seen from an English-centred viewpoint, no doubt it is. From the point of view of Britain, it is not just too simple. It is wrong.

There is nothing inevitable at all about the lasting success of that triumphant event in 1603. It is actually one of the great historical puzzles of the early-modern period that it did survive. It was, after all, only one of a number of dynastic unions, none of which were to survive like this one. The Franco-Polish union of 1573 ended in roaring farce after only eighteen months, with the Franco-Polish king Henry III fleeing across the Polish border to the sound of frantic appeals from one of his Polish subjects, swimming madly up the Vistula. Another Polish union, that with Sweden in 1587, ended not with farce but with irony, as the Swedish king Sigismund Vasa lost his Swedish kingdom. The union of Spain and Portugal began in inauspicious circumstances in 1580, when Philip II enforced his claim to the Portuguese throne by lining up Spanish troops on the border; it ended when the Portuguese seized the chance offered by internal crisis in Spain, and disentangled themselves in 1640. Yet there was a union which seemed to have exactly the reasons for survival which King James was to point out to a hostile English parliament in 1607 when he pleaded that the kingdoms as well as the crowns should be united: in terms of religion, geography and similarity in language, it made sense.[3] These failed unions give grounds for asking how it was that the king who 'made' Britain in 1603 made something which is still with us today; and it suggests that Whig historians may have seriously

3.1. Designs for the new 'British' flag

underestimated King James's place in the history of the developing state not just of England but of Britain.

The success of the 1603 union is, after all, as much a puzzle in British as in European terms. It was not the marriage of two willing, let alone loving partners; it was an arranged political marriage in which, under a thin veneer of harmony, lay bickering and brawling, bitterness and a great deal of resentment and distrust. The English and Scots did not like one another at all. By the late sixteenth century, the Armada and war with Spain had made the Spaniards England's major enemy. But they were the new enemy. The old one lay far closer to home. The English knew, with all the confidence of centuries of tradition, that they were superior to the Scots, in manners, culture, wealth and above all legally – for was not Scotland a vassal kingdom of England? They also knew the much more unpalatable fact that although their greater military power always enabled them to beat Scottish armies – except for one embarrassing battle long ago, Bannockburn in 1314 – they had never managed to conquer Scotland. No wonder they disliked the Scots intensely. And now this inferior and profoundly irritating little nation was likely to provide the next king of England, all because their own great queen had resisted their most reasonable and repeated requests that she should marry and produce a Tudor heir. It was a bitter pill for a people famed for pride in their nationality that the succession should be thus diverted to the descendant of Henry VII's elder daughter Margaret, who had married James IV of Scotland in 1503.

The inferior nation, of course, took a very different view of things. Sixteenth-century Scotland was not the underdog of modern times. That unfortunate and sometimes unattractive animal stands yapping mournfully between us and the kingdom from which the first king of Britain came, and makes it difficult to appreciate the staggering self-confidence of the Scots and of their monarchy. For their centuries of tradition were centuries of successful resistance to *their* 'auld inemie', the English, centuries when they maintained their independence and believed in themselves as one of the major countries of Europe. It had been Henry VII who had taken the initiative in establishing 'Perpetual Peace' with James IV in 1502; the Scottish king was busy anticipating Charles V and dreaming of a Christendom united under his lead against the Turks. The Scots survived the end of that perpetual peace eleven years later, at Flodden. James V beat Henry VIII in the European marriage market; and the minority government of his daughter Mary had resisted Henry VIII's attempts to marry his son Edward to their queen, a scheme pushed first by diplomacy and then by English armies in the 'Rough Wooing' of the 1540s. In 1560 English troops came north again, to aid the Scottish Protestants against the French; their

help resulted in both French and English leaving Scotland, and leaving the Scottish reformers to establish what they later called 'one of the purest kirks under heaven', a kirk which was certainly one of the most assertive on earth, as confidence in the particular favour of God was added to the political confidence of the Scots. Such was the pushy little kingdom which waited for Elizabeth to die and give it the last laugh in the old story of English imperialist ambitions, and waited also for the new pleasures which the Scots assumed would be on offer once their king could tap the wealth of England.

Early seventeenth-century Englishmen were naturally unlikely to appreciate the background from which James came, to see in it any more than barbarity and backwardness. That does not mean that the historian should necessarily agree with them. Yet there is a long historiographical tradition of the boorish, homosexual cowardly pedant, slobbering over his food and his favourites, his clothes monstrously padded because of his fear of the assassin's knife; and such personal failings were not – could not be – redeemed by political skills, for his only experience of rule was in Scotland, where kings were lucky if they survived at all. Almost every aspect of this picture of the king and his northern kingdom is at best burlesque, at worst grotesque caricature. None of James's portraits gives even a hint of the

3.2. The young James VI of Scotland with the effigy of his murdered father

3.3. James VI of
Scotland as a child

appalling creature of popular imagery. It is in fact a literary portrayal, from the bitter and witty pen of an English household official, Anthony Welden. This choleric individual accompanied James on his one visit to Scotland in 1617, and loathed the experience, pouring out his scorn in a work claiming to be *A Perfect Description of the People and Country of Scotland*. *The Perfect Description* included such gems as 'the air might be wholesome but for the stinking people that inhabit it' or, of Scottish women, 'Pride is a thing bred in their bones and their flesh naturally abhors cleanliness; their body smells of sweat and their splay feet never offend in socks. To be chained in marriage with one of them, were to be tied to a dead carcass, and cast into a stinking ditch.' This diatribe cost Weldon his job. His response was to turn his venom against James himself and, in *The Court and Character of King James*, produce the character sketch whose influence has never waned.[4] It is a monument to English xenophobia, not to King James.

The picture of Scotland as peculiarly backward is equally mis-leading. James did have a violent and unstable childhood, by the standards of modern child psychologists; by sixteenth-century standards, it was neither politically nor personally unusual. The civil war which followed Mary's enforced abdication was very small beer compared to the French wars of religion; and the whole minority has much in common with the factional politics of Edward VI's reign and Mary Tudor's accession in England, in which three leading politicians lost their lives, just like three of James's four regents, Moray, Lennox and Morton.

More generally, ruling Scotland was certainly not a simple matter. Very considerable political skills were needed and never more so than in the late sixteenth century. James inherited a tradition of monarchical rule determined by the two unusual features of Stewart kingship in the fifteenth and sixteenth centuries: recurrent minorities and absence of war. Both meant that government pressure on the governed was relatively minimal. There was no successive line of adult kings who could develop royal power in a continual process; instead, reigns of individually very powerful kings were succeeded by periods of minority government. These kings had high opinions of themselves as European monarchs, but they did not normally pursue the military ambitions of the kings of France, Spain and England; neither men nor money were demanded for grandiose undertakings. The result was a successful and stable state which hardly ever exceeded the limits of its own potential, and a monarchy whose remarkable power and prestige came from its position as the focal point of a kingdom in which there was little opposition to it. The key to that success was, and remained in the late sixteenth century, co-operation with the great men of the localities. So what Scottish kingship brings sharply into focus is not

Mars Puer, Aella Virgo, VULPES, Leo, Nullus.

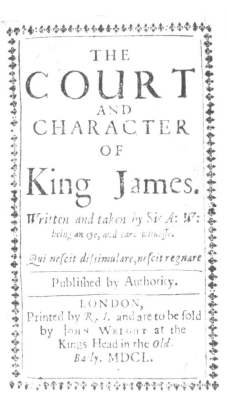

THE
COURT
AND
CHARACTER
OF
King James.

Written and taken by Sir A: W: being an eye, and eare witnesse.

Qui nescit dissimulare, nescit regnare

Published by Authority.

LONDON,
Printed by R. I. and are to be sold by JOHN WRIGHT at the Kings Head in the old Baily. MDCL.

3.4. The Court and Character of King James

the grandeur of monarchy, for it did not rely on great formality or cults of adoration such as Elizabeth encouraged, but the political necessity of being able to manage men; and that lies at the heart of any governmental system, however sophisticated it may be. And because the reality behind the shambling unpleasant pedant whom we know as James VI and I was a casual and approachable man who combined a high sense of his royalty with great skill in discussion and debate, James was one of the greatest exponents of kingship ever to sit on the Scottish throne.[5]

He had need to be; for to inherited traditions were added new problems. Politically and socially, Scotland was changing fast. James ruled a kingdom as much afflicted by the trauma of Reformation as any other in Europe; his greatest political battle was with the extreme presbyterians, followers of Andrew Melville, over the relative powers of church and state.[6] He also had to meet new reactions and expectations. His own extravagance brought regular taxation into Scottish life for the first time; and when a government taxes, then the localities can no longer slumber, and awareness and discontent are born. Moreover, the growth of literacy over the previous century had

3.5. Andrew Melville, Scottish reformer

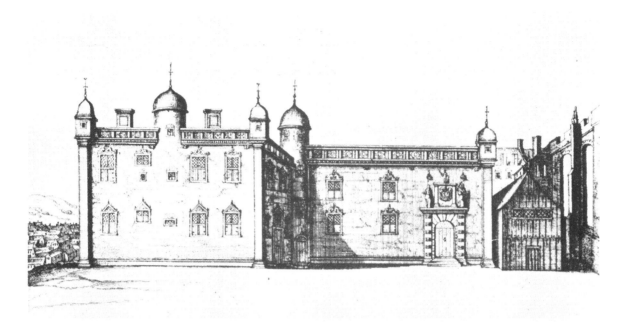

3.6. The Parliament
House in Edinburgh

reached the point where an educated laity demanded its place in the
government's sun; laymen who had previously been concerned with
the affairs of their localities fought for places at the centre, and
political faction was now as much a problem for a Scottish king as for
any other.[7]

The man who succeeded Elizabeth had therefore had twenty years
of successful rule over conflicting factions, lay and religious; he had
presided over parliaments where political and ideological debates were
fought out; and he had survived and beaten off attacks by that vocal
and often virulent body, the General Assembly of the kirk. He had
also had favourites. Two of the four great Jacobean favourites, Esme
Stuart, duke of Lennox, and George, earl of Huntly, flourished before
1603; two, Robert, earl of Somerset, and George, duke of Buckingham,
after it. But in no case was James so besotted by a pretty face and
figure that he became wholly dominated by these men. All held their
place because the king saw them as men of political usefulness as well
as objects of affection; they could be used, in the world of factional
politics, to offset rival political groups or as buffers against the king's
opponents, and never – even in the case of Buckingham – were they
allowed complete control over political decisions or patronage
networks.[8] For this was a man whose sense of office was grounded in
the fact that he had never known what it was like not to be king. And
because he was also a scholar, he wrote about it as king of Scotland in
the late 1590s. He carved out a place for himself in the European
debate about the nature and limitations of royal power, with his

theoretic defence of divine right *The Trew Law of Free Monarchies*, and his masterly practical handbook *Basilikon Doron*.[9] His experience and his ideas make nonsense of the lingering belief that he was not up to ruling the more developed kingdom of England; indeed, compared to the exile who became Henry VII in 1485, or to Mary and Elizabeth, both in the political wilderness as princesses, James emerges as one of the best-trained kings England ever had.

The real trouble in England was that he was a foreigner, and that he was surrounded by 'Scotsmen on the make', whom J.M. Barrie regarded as one of the most impressive sights in the world, but who were simply terrifying to early seventeenth-century Englishmen. The full-throated roar of welcome which greeted him was less one of pure joy than of curiosity and relief, mingled with disquiet. He alone averted the fears of civil war or foreign invasion; hence the relief. But from Sir Robert Cecil and his other new councillors, agonising about his refusal to let them usher him into his new role under their guidance,

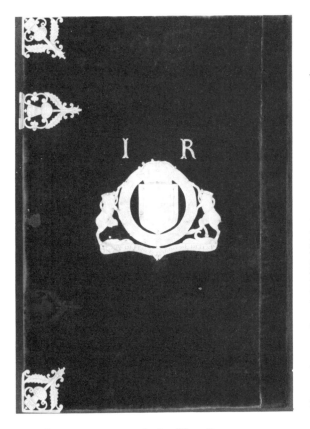

3.7. The cover to James vi's *Basilikon Doron*

3.8. A page from the *Basilikon Doron* showing James's handwriting

to the string of yeomen and artisans indicted for speaking against his accession, the same anxious response can be heard.[10] He roused antagonism because he refused to become wholly identified with English interests, and insisted on drawing on his Scottish experience. He was not greatly interested in Ireland, but his Irish policy – the Plantation of Ulster – was not so much the continuation of Elizabethan policy as a direct consequence of his idea of planting lowland Scots in the highlands, to civilise the clans.[11] His dream of union of the kingdoms dominated the early years of his English rule, and brought only mutual distrust in its wake when it failed; the English disliked everything about it, from his use of the name Britain – which would, they said, confuse foreigners – and his new flag, to his attempts to unify the laws of the two countries and, even worse, to create commercial union which would let the beggarly Scots get their hands on English wealth.[12] When he thought of English matters, he did so in a way very different from his predecessors. He fretted against the institutional barriers which cut him off from the centres of political debate, parliament and council, which he had attended regularly in Scotland. He complained about the English predilection for constitutional niceties and matters of principle, which held up practical decisions and results. That clash of styles showed up right at the beginning of the reign, in the first exchange of letters between James and his English council. James told the councillors to thank God for the blessing of the king about to come among them, and meanwhile instructed them to keep government going in England. His horrified councillors had little time to think about God, in the panic of sending messengers north to tell him that English government could no longer function because he had not used the right form of words to authorise them to act.[13] Xenophobia and a very different approach came between him and his English subjects. It made his position as king of three kingdoms look very fragile, and the future of the composite kingdoms bleak.

And yet the union survived distrust and hostility. Why? To begin with, even the Scottish James had redeeming features from the English point of view. Despite his disturbing political theory, he was in practice less autocratic and far less interventionist than Elizabeth. His direct personal style may have irritated, but it also did something to reduce, for a time, the weight of institutionalism which burdened English government. *Rex Pacificus*, with his motto 'Beati Pacifici', provided a breathing-space from war; not all approved his policy, but it took strains off the localities which had been visible in the 1590s and were to become so again in the early years of Charles I. His church was open to more shades of opinion, including the moderate Puritans, than it had been under Elizabeth or would be under Charles;

the beauty of the language of the Authorised Version of the Bible is a fitting tribute to the Jacobean church and the aspirations of its head.[14] For these reasons, he did in time come to command not only respect but also affection from his English subjects; the moving little account of the enthusiasm with which the aging king was greeted when he came to open parliament in 1621, his own cheerfulness and affability – despite the fact that he was too weak to walk – suggest something very different from the clamouring, staring crowds of 1603.[15]

Behind the personal achievement lay another crucial factor. Like another successful union of the crowns, that of Poland and Lithuania in 1385 which led to the incorporating union of 1569, it was the ruler of the lesser, not the greater, power who united the crowns; and that, despite all the tensions and difficulties, produced a political and social balance which was to prove remarkably resilient. What James did, between 1603 and 1625, was to buy time; his reign of almost a quarter of a century gave time for union to become established fact, without either side finding that they were unduly hurt by it. The Scots did not yet feel swallowed up by the larger kingdom; they might have lost their king, but he was still their king, known to and interested in them, and the pride they could take in having given England a king survived English rebuffs so long as James lived. Moreover, the tradition of looking beyond Scotland played its part in the Scottish perception of the union of the crowns. Leading Scotsmen like the earl of Dunbar genuinely tried to assimilate themselves to the English political world, and could do so with some tact; in 1610 it was Dunbar who persuaded the king not to react with ferocity to a demonstration of anti-Scottish feeling in the English Parliament.[16] In this reign, the idea of the London-Scot was born. James's brilliant circle of court poets came south and began to write in the new medium of English; one, Alexander Craig, called himself 'Scoto-Britane' and even 'Banffo-Britane'.[17] The English suffered the initial psychological shock of finding themselves ruled by a king who was not exclusively interested in them and their ways, an experience they had not had since the early thirteenth century. But James showed sufficient interest for them to recover their sense of superiority and find things to praise as well as to blame in their Scottish king – and in any case they could look forward to having a wholly English king again once he was dead, for there was little to make his sons identify themselves with Scotland. Hence their adoration of James's overrated heir Henry, and the popularity which Charles enjoyed in the last years of the reign.

When James VI and I is divided into his two halves, and treated as separate kings of Scotland and England, then his reputation as king of Scotland will always stand higher than his reputation as king of

3.9. A medal of James VI
and I.

England. But that is not how he should be judged. For James VI and I
was a unique phenomenon. He was the only genuine exponent of dual
monarchy who ever sat on the British throne. The union he created
did not run smoothly for ever afterwards. However, the historical
accident which brought a Scottish king to the English throne, and the
passionate belief of that king that it was possible to rule composite
kingdoms, and provide good rule for both, laid a remarkably firm
foundation; for all the later vicissitudes, there was never to be a
sufficient consensus, on either side of the border, that the union should
be broken. That owes a very great deal to the curious but very
impressive skills of the first king of Britain. Like Mozart, he was laid
to rest in an unmarked grave. But there is one memorial: the glorious
Rubens ceiling in the Banqueting House of Whitehall, depicting union,
peace and harmony, and even an expression of bewilderment on the
face of the central figure of King James, which, in view of his

problems and his achievements in dealing with them, is somehow very appropriate.

Further reading

Letters of King James VI *and* I, ed. G.P.V. Akrigg (Berkeley and London, 1984); G. Donaldson, *Scotland: James* V–*James* VII (Edinburgh, 1965); M. Lee Jr, *Government by Pen: Scotland under James* VI *and* I (Urbana, 1980); R. Lockyer, *Buckingham* (London, 1981); C. Russell, *The Crisis of Parliaments* (Oxford, 1971) and *Parliaments and English Politics 1621–1629* (Oxford, 1979); *Faction and Parliament: Essays on Early Stuart History*, ed. K. Sharpe (Oxford, 1978); *The Reign of James* VI *and* I, ed. A.G.R. Smith (London, 1973); D.H. Willson, *King James* VI *and* I (London, 1956); J. Wormald, *Court, Kirk and Community: Scotland 1470–1625* (London, 1981).

CHAPTER FOUR

Crown and Parliament

Kevin Sharpe

In 1649, Charles I lost his head on the scaffold at Whitehall, and the institution of monarchy was abolished by dictate of parliament. How had the government of England arrived at such a crisis? Were the events of 1649 the outcome of problems within the institution of monarchy itself, or had the personal actions of Charles I led to the destruction of the crown as well as his own death? The answer to such questions divides historians now as it did the men of the seventeenth century who fought the Civil War. But the explanation for the traumatic events of the 1640s undoubtedly lies both in the nature of government and in the character of the king.

The government of seventeenth-century England was still government by personal monarchy. That is to say, the king in his own person was the fount of all the power and authority that today is invested in the prime minister, the cabinet and parliament, as well as the queen. Indeed the daily administration of business, domestic as well as foreign affairs, the maintenance of law and order, the protection of the church and the supervision of local government, were all the king's responsibility. The king too was the ultimate court of appeal: to him came petitions, complaints and legal problems, for his favour, clemency and judgement. Some judges were to state in the famous legal cases of the early seventeenth century that the king was the source of the law, even that the king's word *was* the law.[1]

This is not to say that even in theory the power of the king was unlimited. In the medieval English past there were precedents of monarchs whose overwhelming exercise of authority had been curtailed (as King John, at Runnymede), kings who had been deposed (as Richard II), even brutally murdered (as Edward II). Constitutional theory and political ideas in England had reflected the limitations to as well as the scope of royal authority. In the fifteenth century the

4.1. The execution of Charles I

political theorist Sir John Fortescue had described the government of England as a *dominium politicum et regale*, as a mixed polity in which the king ruled in co-operation with his leading subjects, and in accordance with the law. Parliaments in England, as early Stuart antiquaries frequently pointed out, were of the most ancient establishment. By the sixteenth century too, *statute* law, law made by the king, Lords and Commons in parliament, had become established as the supreme legislative authority.

However the Tudor century, for all the enhanced importance of parliament, undoubtedly saw a greater emphasis upon the powers and prerogative of the crown.[2] There were a number of reasons for this. The anarchy of the Wars of the Roses inclined the magnates to favour a strong monarchy as the guarantee of order and privilege. The break from Rome made Henry VIII head of the church as well as the state and so endowed the crown with ecclesiastical as well as secular authority. The persistent threat of foreign invasion throughout the sixteenth century – by the pope, France, Scotland and then Spain – led men to recognise the need for strong leadership. The combination of these factors, together with the skilful dissemination of patronage to powerful men and a powerful insistence on obedience preached from the pulpit, led to an obsession with order and to the recognition of the monarch as the sovereign power of the realm, the keystone of the arch of all order and government.[3] By the late sixteenth century we find writers such as Thomas Hooker describing the queen as an absolute monarch. By 1603 James I's claim to rule by divine right was not extraordinary; it was the statement of a commonplace.[4]

The early Stuart kings had immense theoretical power, the importance of which should not be underestimated. But this theoretical power had very little practical backing. They possessed neither the machinery of government nor the force of arms to ensure obedience. Unlike their European counterparts, Philip III of Spain or Henry IV and Louis XIII of France, James I and Charles I depended for troops upon the retainers and followers that their noble subjects could raise from their estates and localities; and upon an often ramshackle 'homeguard' of county militiamen, consisting of peasants grudgingly mustered, ill-trained and equipped, and understandably reluctant to fight, especially beyond the confines of their county.[5] Nor did the Stuarts, at least until the very end of the seventeenth century, have anything that we might recognise as a bureaucracy or civil service, either in Whitehall or in the localities.

Most officials of central government – from the Lord Treasurer and secretaries of state down – depended on gifts, perks and bribes rather than wages.[6] The officers of local government, justices of the peace, sheriffs, lord and deputy lieutenants enjoyed only the honour of local status for their (considerable) pains. And the hundred and parish constables, often faced with levying unpopular rates on their neighbours, were denied even that. This was obviously not a very efficient way to run a government but the Stuarts had no option. They could not afford a professional civil service. By 1625 the Stuart crown was near bankruptcy.

This was not a new problem. But it was a problem that had not become as apparent in the sixteenth century, indeed a problem that might have been solved then. For Henry VIII, in addition to his Tudor lands, had inherited the vast estates of the Yorkists and Lancastrians, and he added to them the rich lands of the monasteries dissolved in 1536. The income from these lands could have made the crown financially self-sufficient. Instead, Henry's wars with France depleted his inheritance and Elizabeth's conflict with Spain and her campaigns in Ireland all but consumed what was left. Taxation granted by parliament offered no solution to the problem. Parliament still expected to grant subsidies only for war and such like emergencies. Moreover, the yield of the subsidies granted was falling, significantly in actual sums and catastrophically in real terms during a period of very high inflation. At the time that the business of government was expanding, and the costs of warfare rocketing, the resources of the English crown were decreasing.[7] The early Stuarts had all the theoretical power of their continental counterparts, but they lacked the military force, the bureaucracy and the money necessary at times to translate it into practice.

Monarchical government in early Stuart England, then, rested not upon resources or force, but necessarily upon co-operation – between the king and the most important landed nobles and gentry of the realm. In return for royal patronage – honours, offices, pensions or posts – the nobility and gentry governed the localities in the king's service. For the most part the system, if a series of such personal relationships merits the name, worked well. But there were limitations to such co-operation: loyalty to self, family, estates or locality might compete with, as well as complement that to the crown; personal beliefs and private commitments might at times conflict with royal policy. Successful monarchical government depended upon a sensitive skill in the art of winning compliance, upon the delicate conduct of relationships with powerful and proud men, upon the maintenance of a personal identity of interest between the king and his propertied subjects. To see this is to recognise that the stability of personal monarchy depended very much upon the person of the king.

In succeeding peacefully to the crowns of his father as a mature young Englishman of twenty-five, never having doubted his succession since the death of his brother, Henry, Charles I was the exceptional monarch of the Tudor and Stuart centuries. His predecessors had snatched their crowns in battle, fought off dynastic challenge or rebellions, been minors, women or a foreigner. Charles was also unique as the first heir to *three* kingdoms: to the crown of Scotland as well as those of England and Ireland. The year of his succession, 1625, marked something of a high point of personal monarchy: there were no dynastic threats to the Stuart line; England had been free of the riots and rebellions endemic in Europe, and had been spared the violence and heat of religious controversy and war. At twenty-five, newly betrothed to the princess of France, Charles I could realistically have anticipated a glorious reign.

It was, perhaps, just such an inheritance, as well as the king's reserved and formal disposition, that was to stamp a very different style upon the reign, and see a far less happy outcome than that which all anticipated. It is perhaps important that Charles' profound sense of the dignity and majesty of kingship had never been tempered by the political need to manoeuvre or struggle in order to enjoy it. The reverence and deference paid to him as king of England had never been, as in the case of his father, compromised by the more familiar and casual exchange with subjects that characterised the Scottish court.[8] Rather the young prince's experience of the gravity and decorum of the Spanish court (to which he had travelled in romantic incognito in 1623 in order to win the Infanta as his bride) had enhanced his natural inclination to aloof grandeur, and sharpened his repulsion for the more casual style of his father. In many respects Charles I, more than any of his predecessors, was England's supreme Renaissance prince: his personal style (and within weeks that ordered for his court) was majestic, sophisticated and cultivated. The paintings of Van Dyck, vividly portraying a king calm and confident ruling unquestioned a country harmonious and peaceful, encapsulate both the man and his vision of monarchy. Like the paintings, the court rituals and royal entertainments presented the royal belief that the polity might be transformed into that ideal commonwealth by the power of the king's person and example.[9]

4.2. Charles I

Chaste, sober and unextravagant, desirous of the best for his people and devoted to the duties of his place, most of all, a divinely anointed king, Charles I could never understand the need to justify or explain his actions, nor comprehend why any would have needed to dispute or question them. He was *not* autocratic: Charles listened to a wide range of advice, consulted his Privy Council on all matters and often read dispatches and briefs carefully. But once he had made up his mind, once he had grasped a principle or determined upon a policy, the political process of debate and persuasion stopped as far as he was concerned. The royal order once delivered was for immediate action. Co-operation and loyalty were qualities Charles expected, rather than saw any need to win.[10] In itself such a personality need not have proved a problem: most monarchs expected loyal service and, for the most part, the *spirit* of royal orders was carried out in the context of local and individual circumstances. What was different about Charles was his insistence upon the *letter* as well as the spirit of a decree. He established above all an obsessive concern for preciseness, for exactness, for uniformity – not only throughout his realm of England, but in his other kingdoms as well.

It was in his methods rather than his aims or policies that Charles I proved a radical break with his father. Where James proceeded slowly, with caution and by diplomacy, be it in his desire to bring the Scottish kirk more in line with the Church of England, or in his subtle diplomatic negotiations with Spain, Charles acted with precipitation. The determination and energy of the new king were soon felt both at the centre of government and in the localities, as Charles set up commissions to reform the royal household and issued directives to improve the militia. Events added urgency to a natural precipitation. If the move towards greater efficiency was powered by the king's personality, it was also accelerated by the necessities of war.

For Charles I's reign opened with war, first with Spain and then with France. Initially the war was popular: since the days of the Armada, Catholic Spain had been regarded as the principal threat to the security of Protestant England. But English offensives petered out through inadequate supplies, rotten food and provisions, and ill-trained men. The wars of 1625–8 were a military and diplomatic disaster and they became too a disaster for stability and harmony of government in England. By 1628 the wars had greatly strained the relationships between King Charles and his subjects represented in parliament. On their part members of parliament expressed their discontent at the expenses and their frustrations at the failures of the war which had not materialised as the Protestant crusades against the popish Spaniards of their rhetoric. They blamed the king's leading minister and favourite, the duke of Buckingham, for mismanagement;

they presented as grievances against the liberties and properties of Englishmen the emergency measures necessitated by the war: the raising of extraordinary fiscal levies, the pressing of men, and the billeting of troops on households. Charles I, for his part, frustrated at their reluctance adequately to finance the war for which they had clamoured, blamed his parliament for the mortal blow to his honour inflicted by failure. In short, the demands and chaos of the war years undermined the trust between the king and his subjects.[11] As some members of parliament voiced fears that Charles had shown himself

4.3. George Villiers, duke of Buckingham

inclined to govern arbitrarily, so the truculence of their complaints against what he saw as necessary measures transformed Charles' devotion to order into an obsession and turned him from an inclination to rule with parliament to a belief that he could only govern effectively without them. Most significantly, this naturally resolute man became a monarch determined to pursue certain principles and policies – whatever the circumstances and obstacles, and whatever the grumblings and discontents they aroused.

In 1629, however, when Charles dissolved his last parliament for eleven years, there was no indication of the storms that were to come. In many ways there were good prospects for a new start. The duke of Buckingham, the minister who had become the scapegoat for the ills of the realm, had been assassinated in 1628 and there was widespread optimism at the king's taking the reins of government into his own hands. Secondly, the peace concluded with France and Spain by 1630 eased the tensions created by the wars. The king's and Privy Council's vigorous actions to deal with recent harvest failures and with poor relief were welcomed by a local magistracy always fearful of popular riot and rebellion. Charles hoped to demonstrate to his subjects his good intentions for the government of the country.

The decade of Charles' 'personal rule' from 1629 to 1640 is the period in which we may best see the king's attempts to translate his ideals for the government of the realm into practice.[12] Proclamations, letters and directives were issued, and levies and rates were raised in an attempt to improve local government, fashion an effectual or 'exact' militia and build a powerful navy. Detailed reports and censuses were requested in order to ascertain that orders had been carried out.

Charles' obsession with order ranged from regulations governing the size of building bricks in London to measures to establish religious uniformity in all three kingdoms. Most of Charles' *policies* were not unpopular: many men recognised the need for a strong navy in the midst of the Thirty Years War; most, in England at least, were devoted to the prayer book and the liturgies of the Church of England. But the constantly hectoring tone, the rigorous pursuit of objectives by the Privy Council and in the secular and ecclesiastical courts undoubtedly aroused antagonism. The gentry of the localities, charged with the execution of royal orders and faced with a barrage of directives, had occasion to bristle at what they saw as unwarranted interference in their affairs, as well as cause for complaint at the new administrative burdens on top of the 'stacks of statutes' for the enforcement of which they were already responsible. Rates such as Ship Money, issued to finance the fleet, and the drive for uniformity in church services ran roughshod over local circumstances and customs.[13]

Charles I's concept of order could not accommodate that variety of practice or worship, the turning of a blind eye to occasional misdemeanours, that rather loose interpretation of order that characterised English government in church and state. Nor could it tolerate diversity among the three kingdoms over which he ruled.

In seeking to bring the religious and secular governments of Scotland and Ireland more in line with that of England, Charles was by no means an untypical ruler: James I had desired no less. But James I had always remained a Scottish king as well as king of Scotland. He knew his Scottish lords and worked through skilfully established personal relationships in order gradually to effect his aims. Charles I determined to rule his three kingdoms from Whitehall. He never went to Ireland and did not return to the Scotland of his birth for his coronation until eight years after his succession. In consequence, the prayer book that he ordered to be used by the kirk, not widely disliked in itself, was widely resented as an English imposition, as indeed the king's attempted reform of Scottish government stimulated fear of an assault upon the status and privileges of the aristocracy in Scotland.[14] As in England, Charles saw no need to explain his intentions. He showed considerable concern that the channels of government flowed fluently out from Whitehall, but he did too little to ensure that the reactions, the local problems and reports of discontents, flowed as freely back.[15]

It was, perhaps, his insensitivity to and ignorance of the reactions to his policies that was Charles I's greatest failing as monarch of all his kingdoms. It is difficult for historians today to conclude about the local responses to these policies. It was difficult too for the king, especially in the absence of parliaments, which served as occasions for the expression of grievances, to be informed of them. Levies were paid, the militia was improved, dilapidated churches were beautified, but how grudgingly we cannot say. Even when they questioned the wisdom or legality of Charles' demands, the gentry were reluctant to oppose them and thereby set an example of disobedience to their inferiors. Certainly there was no sign in 1637 of the political crisis that was to plunge England into civil war.[16] But the outbreak of rebellion in Scotland was undoubtedly a sign of troubles. Not for the first time, Charles was to discover that the theoretical power of the monarchy was not matched by the capacity to enforce it with ease.

It was the campaign against the Scots from 1637 that brought this home to Charles once again and demonstrated how far his achievements had fallen short of his ideals. It was also the campaign against the Scots that raised again the problems of 1625–8. In the localities the preparations for war added costs and demands for money and men considerably greater than the levies already being

4.4. Charles I outside Edinburgh

raised.[17] Urgent business was now heaped upon already overpressed local officials. A natural reluctance of trained (and pressed) men to fight was fostered by skilful Scots propaganda which pointed to dangerous innovations in church and state counselled by popish advisers who intended the same for England.[18] Not that the Scots were popular: they were old enemies of the English and the partial union of the two realms under James VI and I had, if anything,

4.5. The Commons in 1640

sharpened rather than muted their hostility. Had the war against the Scots been brief, successful and glorious, Charles might well have raised his political credit by it; but 'war' proved a failure without even a battle being fought. As the soldiers returned home unpaid, and the costs of a fruitless campaign were counted, resentment mounted. Justices and deputy lieutenants feared that new central demands for Ship Money and war supplies were threatening local order. The gentry demanded a parliament in order to explain to an all-too-ignorant king and Council the problems which they encountered in their counties.

The parliament that convened at Westminster in the spring of 1640 was by no means in revolutionary mood.[19] Like the king himself, they believed that they had assembled to air grievances *and* to vote subsidies for the war. But the order of these priorities divided them. Charles (and some MPs) urged immediate supply, promising a longer session to hear the Commons' complaints. But other MPs were anxious *first* to see their grievances redressed, and most feared for the reaction in their localities if taxes were voted without some relief from the extraordinary levies of the last decade. To many members of parliament Charles' demand for urgent grants of supply to fight a war over which (unusually in English history), they had not been consulted, was unreasonable.[20] To the king, however, and no less understandably, the debates and delays of the Commons, in the midst of war, confirmed all his suspicions of their dilatoriness and uselessness. After three weeks he dissolved them.

During the summer of 1640 government all but collapsed. The Scots invaded Newcastle and Charles was not able to resist them. Ship Money was not paid; law and order dissolved in the localities. During the months of chaos and uncertainty, rumours had begun to circulate of Catholic conspirators plotting to undermine Protestantism in England as in Scotland. When a parliament was recalled in November it met in an atmosphere of fear which subsequent events were to turn into hysteria. Fear and hysteria were not the best climates for the making of a political settlement. That most MPs wanted a return to normality seems clear. And that Charles was now prepared to conciliate and compromise cannot be denied; the legislation of the first months of the Long Parliament, removing the fiscal levies and dismantling courts through which Charles had financed and enforced his rule, met with no royal opposition. However, the possibilities of settlement were complicated by the presence of a Scottish army which necessitated as well as guaranteed the continued sitting of parliament and which was to demand a religious settlement to which Charles I and a good number of MPs could not consent. Problems in two kingdoms became a crisis in all three when the Irish Catholics rose in rebellion in October 1641, confirming the fears of plots fostered by a popish cabal, which, it was now believed, had even infiltrated the court. Amidst fears and rumours the trust which is essential for any political settlement dissolved. When he was denied the trust of his subjects that he thought his due, Charles decided to re-establish his authority by force.[21]

Charles I was not a despotic ruler bent on the subversion of the English constitution or the erection of an absolute monarchy on the French pattern. He was an arch conservative in his aims and

4.6. Charles and
Henrietta Maria dining
at court

intentions; he looked back to what he saw as an earlier stability in the
reign of Henry VIII, rather than forward or abroad to the France of
Louis XIV. But Charles I learned too late that personal loyalty and
service were fostered by carefully cultivated personal relationships: that
loyalty and service, especially in difficult times, needed to be wooed
and won rather than assumed. English government depended upon the
willing co-operation of the unpaid local gentry and, in turn, upon
their capacity to maintain the authority of the crown and the law in
their provinces. Perhaps Charles I never fully understood that securing
their co-operation involved tolerating at times the laziness natural to
unpaid gentlemen who sought their place to enhance their honour
rather than to be full-time administrators, and tolerating often the
adjustment of central orders to local circumstances and interests. It
was not least because he learned too late to court men and never to
tolerate such inefficiencies that Charles alienated many of the most
powerful men of the realm, and ultimately lost his life and his crown.

Further reading

C. Russell (ed.), *The Origins of the English Civil War* (Oxford, 1971);
C. Russell, *Parliaments and English Politics 1621–29* (Oxford, 1979);
J.S. Morrill, *The Revolt of the Provinces* (London, 1980); K. Sharpe
(ed.), *Faction and Parliament* (Oxford, 1978); H.C. Tomlinson (ed.),
Before the English Civil War (London, 1983); P. Gregg, *Charles I*
(London, 1981); *C. Carlton, Charles I: The Personal Monarch*
(London, 1983); Anthony Fletcher, *The Outbreak of the English Civil
War* (London, 1981).

'For King and Country'

Ronald Hutton

There is a story, very popular in recent decades, of a farmer on Marston Moor, who was working in a field in July 1644, when the armies arrived to fight the biggest battle of the English Civil War. On being told that the quarrel was between king and parliament, he replied 'What, has they two fallen out again?' Unfortunately, the incident is not recorded in any contemporary source. The Civil War was just not that sort of war. For almost two years our farmer would have had to send money and supplies to a garrison at York, seven miles away. Soldiers would continually have crossed his lands. For the past two months he would have been forced to give money and food to a huge army besieging York. His horses would probably have been taken too, and he would have been lucky if his cottage had not been plundered bare. This was, in brief, not a conflict that anybody could either not know about or could ignore. In fact, it was because the people were dragged reluctantly into it and loathed it, that it was eventually halted.

It was arguably the most terrible experience that the English and Welsh people have ever undergone, dividing them bitterly and threatening almost every assumption that they had made about their world. It happened because the most respected institution in the country, parliament, split in half. On one side was King Charles I and most of the Lords, on the other the majority of the House of Commons. What had gone wrong was a collapse of trust. The leaders of the Commons (and some peers) believed that unless firm constitutional restraints were placed upon the king, then he would pursue authoritarian policies in church and state and destroy those who had tried to restrain him. Charles denied this charge and accused his opponents of depriving him of his just rights to consolidate their own political power. There was some truth upon both sides.

A true and exact Relation of the manner of his Maiesties setting up of His Standard at *Nottingham*, on Munday the 22. of Augu∫t 1642.

Fir∫t, The forme of the Standard, as it is here figured, and who were present at the advancing of it

Secondly, The danger of ∫etting up of former Standards, and the damage
which en∫ued thereon.

Thirdly, A relation of all the Standards that ever were ∫et up by any King.

Fourthly, the names of tho∫e Knights who are appointed to be the Kings
Standard-bearers. With the forces that are appoynted to guard it.

Fifthly, The manner of the Kings comming fir∫t to *Coventry*.

Sixtly, The *Cavaliers* re∫olution and dangerous threats which they have
uttered, if the King concludes a peace without them, or hearkens unto
his great Councell the Parliament : Moreover how they have ∫hared
and divided *London* among∫t them∫elves already.

When the Commons gained control of London in early 1642, the king moved into the provinces and commanded them to support him. His opponents ordered them to resist his directives. The effect upon the realm of these two powerful and mutually contradictory commands was, to a great extent, that of a hammer hitting a rock; it fractured, but along the lines of pre-existing weakness. Out of this complex of divisions, the rival parties were formed. During the last great collapse of central government, the Wars of the Roses nearly two hundred years before, in the fifteenth century, fighting had been relatively brief and most communities barely touched by it. Floods had caused more disruption. In the intervening period the whole country had become increasingly bound into a single political machine and a common national culture. More and more gentry participated in government, were educated at university and Inns of Court, went to London to conduct business and recorded national news in their diaries. Commoners increasingly responded to general issues at parliamentary elections. This tendency promised a better integrated and more orderly nation, but there was a drawback. If most of the provinces had become enmeshed in a uniform system, then a disturbance at the centre would rebound upon all areas, and a break would be duplicated in all. This is exactly what occurred.

The most important single line of division was over religion, and without this the war would never have been as long and terrible as it was. This was an age in which people in most countries killed each other over the way in which they wished to worship, and the English were no exception. Those who wanted a church stripped of pomp, ritual and ornament, based firmly upon preaching and scripture, tended to support parliament (as the party of the king's enemies termed itself). Those who wanted deference, ceremony and catechism, and the Roman Catholics, tended to support Charles. But the religious factor was only the greatest among several. Another was social tension, for more nobles and leading gentry tended to be royalist than parliamentarian. Clearly, the party which stressed hierarchy more strongly appealed most to the traditional leaders of society.

It is important, nevertheless, to remember that while the major issues at stake were not those of class, but of religion and the extent of royal power, other issues were purely local. In some counties, such as Cheshire and Somerset, the split followed the line of pre-war local political factions. Others followed the lead of a popular resident aristocrat, such as the royalist earl of Derby in Lancashire or the parliamentarian earl of Warwick in Essex. At Chester and Newcastle, the ruling clique became royalists and those who coveted their power parliamentarians. Celtic Wales and the Lake District, remote regions, supported the king as the older and more potent symbol of authority. Some individuals even took wholly rational political decisions, based on the available evidence. Such was the Welsh gentleman Sir Thomas Salusbury, who wrote to a friend to say that he had read Charles' declarations, pondered the role of monarchy in scripture, history and the modern world, and decided to join the king. He added that he was going at once, because he was sure that otherwise his friends would talk him out of it. He did, and soon died of camp fever.

It was a hammer-blow that could break the strongest bonds. It shattered many friendships and several families, and caused old enemies to work together. Local leaders who had persecuted Roman Catholics for a generation now gave them arms, and tenants who had hated their landlords sometimes supported the same side as those lords, nonetheless.

But there were also turncoats in this conflict. Several gentry changed sides in the course of the war for a variety of reasons. Few did so as blatantly as the royalist garrison of Lindisfarne, which sat out the first

5.2. Sir Thomas Salusbury and his family

year of war and then, when an enemy warship appeared, declared for parliament in exchange for a year's pay. Furthermore, and this is very important, the model also fails to take into account the fact that the majority of the population, faced with the contradictory orders of king and parliament, tried to ignore both and stay out of trouble.

In each county from a third to two-thirds of the gentry seem to have taken no active part in the war, and it must be presumed that neither did an even greater proportion of commoners. Many of those counted as partisans were actually forced to assist one group of activists and so were automatically treated as enemies by the other. In most cases neutralism meant passivity, obedience to whichever party happened to be in control of the area. But in twenty-one counties it also took an active form, the community raising vigilantes to keep royalists or Roundhead soldiers out, or the rival parties themselves making pacts to suspend hostilities in their home areas. In every case, these attempts to opt out of the war collapsed, because the English and Welsh had become so used to obeying central government that they simply found themselves incapable of defying both king and parliament.

Moreover, the female half of the population contributed nothing to the outbreak of war. Women did fight once hostilities began, the wives of gentry commanding garrisons and female commoners defending walls with an energy as effective as that of the menfolk. But in all of these cases they were dealing with military situations in which they had been placed by males. By contrast, women at times definitely took the initiative in actions to halt the war or oppose its demands. At Bristol they threw open the city gates to prevent citizens resisting an approaching regiment at the opening of the conflict, while at Derby, near the end of it, they organised and led a riot against war taxation. Such was the complexity of people's response to the war itself that it might seem surprising that the conflict began at all. How did hostilities actually start?

When king and parliament made their appeals to the leaders of cities and counties, a few in each community responded. They put up private money to attract men into regiments, offering princely sums as the struggle was expected to be short. Their agents went through towns and villages like the one described at Myddle, Shropshire: 'With a paper in his hand and three or four soldiers, pikes stuck in the ground besides him', proclaiming that his officers paid 4s 4d a week.[1] From greed, personal loyalty or personal conviction, thousands of men responded to such offers. Once they were drawn together and armed from private or public magazines, they simply took over local capitals and turned them into garrisons, whatever the inhabitants thought of the matter. This experience would have lasted only a few months had, as everybody anticipated, the war been decided by the

5.3. The Battle of Edgehill

first great battle. When that battle came, at Edgehill, it cost about 5000 lives but the net result was merely to render both armies too weak to attack each other again for a long while. Military accident, and not natural allegiance, had made parliament dominant in southern and eastern England, and Charles in the North, Wales and the Midlands. Both sides now prepared for a struggle of attrition, and the country was for the first time properly mobilised for a war effort.

In the course of the whole four-year conflict, perhaps a quarter of the entire adult male population became soldiers. Upon both sides pay was soon in arrears, troops began to desert and conscription was introduced. In action, wounds were caused by blows from clubs and musket-butts, stabs and slices from the blades of pikes, swords and knives, and (most feared) the impact of lead shot from muskets and cannon. A musket-ball could tear through organs and shatter bones, a cannon ball could remove whole limbs and pulp torsos. Sometimes veterans were placed at the rear of raw troops ordered to attack a strong position, with orders to shoot those who tried to turn back. Out of action, many soldiers died of diseases rife in their overcrowded quarters.

The war had its lighter side. Inexperience resulted in some farcical incidents, such as one in Yorkshire when some royalists, bombarding an enemy position, blew up a powder magazine and became so terrified that they threw down their weapons and ran. In the North Midlands, rival garrisons settled down to fight a 'phoney war', collecting money on alternate days to avoid meeting each other. But in general the conflict conformed to the pattern discerned by a Frenchman in his own country's Wars of Religion: 'We fought the first year like angels, the second like men, and the third like devils'.

Few behaved more like angels than the two generals who opposed each other at the battle of Landsdowne in 1643. Before the war they

5.4. Sir William Waller

had been close friends and comrades in arms, and as the armies approached each other, the royalist, Sir Ralph Hopton, wrote to the parliamentarian, Sir William Waller, asking for a meeting. He received the following reply:

> Certanly my affections for you are so unchangeable, that hostility itself cannot violate my friendship to your person, but I must be true to the cause wherein I serve. . . . That great God, which is the searcher of my heart, knows with what a sad sense I go upon this service, and with what a perfect hatred I detest this war without an enemy. . . . We are both upon the stage and must act out those parts which are assigned us in this tragedy; let us do it in a way of honour, and without personal animosities, whatever the issue.[2]

Such nobility was exceptional, and became more so. The corrosive effect of war may be illustrated from the letters of parliament's most famous general, Oliver Cromwell. The earliest was written in May 1643, during his first independent operation:

> For after we had stood a little, above musket shot the one body from the other, they not advancing towards us we agreed to charge them . . . by God's providence they were immediately routed, and all ran away.[3]

Here we are still in the world in which soldiers are routed by exploding magazines. The two forces meet, and just look at each other. After some argument, Cromwell's band decides to do something, and their opponents flee at once. How different is the second letter, from July 1644, after the battle of Marston Moor:

> We never charged but we routed the enemy . . . God made them stubble to our swords . . . Sir, God hath taken away your eldest son by a cannon shot. It broke his thigh, which we were necessitated to cut off, whereof he died. Before his death he told me that . . . he sorrowed, that God had not suffered him any more to be the executioner of His enemies.[4]

The royalists are now depersonalised ('stubble') or demonic ('His enemies') and all this poor, mutilated, dying boy can regret is that he did not kill more of them. The third letter concerns the storming of Drogheda, an Irish town held by English royalist officers in 1649:

> The enemy made three entrenchments, both to the right and left of which we entered: all of which they were forced to quit. Being thus

5.5. The storming of
Drogheda

entered we refused them quarter, having the day before summoned
the town. I believe we put to the sword the whole number of the
defendents.[5]

The killing has become mechanical. A town is offered terms, its
governor refuses, it is stormed and its garrison is killed, as if by a
natural process.

At its worst, the Civil War could be very nasty indeed. When a
parliamentarian castle at Hopton, Herefordshire, was captured in
March 1644, the prisoners were butchered literally like sheep: tied up
and laid on the ground so that their throats could be cut one by one
before they were thrown into a pit. When the royalist general Sir
Richard Grenville captured an enemy foraging party in Devon, he
offered freedom to any one of them prepared to hang his comrades.
When a man actually took up the offer, Sir Richard kept his part of
the bargain and released him, laughing, as soon as the rest had choked
to death. As the victorious Roundheads thundered into the royalist
camp after the battle of Naseby, they found many female civilians
there, wives and lovers of their opponents. Maddened by bloodlust
and hate, they mutilated the faces of these women with their knives.
However, such horrors were as rare as the moments of gallantry. For
most soldiers the drawbacks of military life were hunger, cold, tedium
and fear, compensated for to some, and at certain moments, by the

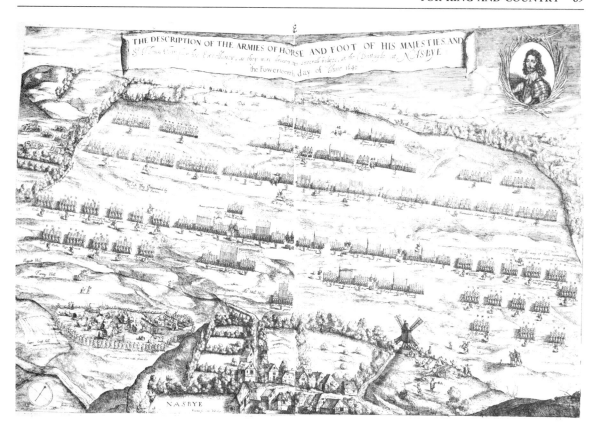

5.6. The Battle of
Naseby, with detail
(right)

intoxication of victory and the profit of plunder.

The universal civilian experience of the conflict consisted of paying for it, in rates or taxes imposed by the party in control of an area. If the region were peaceful, this money was collected by civilian officials, but in war zones soldiers themselves rounded up the cash and supplies upon which they depended. Thus the parish constable of Elmley Lovett, Worcestershire, once received a demand for his village's arrears within three days 'at your perils of pillaging and your houses fired and your persons imprisoned'.[6] The country people of the nearby Evesham area got an order to produce six months' rates within a week, failing which they were 'to expect an unsanctified body of horse amongst you, from which if you hide yourselves (as I believe each of you hath your hole) they shall fire your houses without mercy, hang up your bodies wherever they find them and scare your ghosts.'[7]

This was a taxation of a weight and regularity never known before: every month it removed about a fifth of a propertied person's pre-war income, and that income would anyway have shrunk, in some places drastically, with the disruption of the fighting. On top of this would come irregular levies made to repair the fortifications of towns or to cover the expenses of a convoy passing through the area. In addition, many householders had soldiers billeted on them, who needed bedding, food and fuel.

The cost of this was in theory (but seldom in practice) reimbursed. Even if it were repaid, it consumed the resources upon which taxation was based. This was even more true of the seizure of horses, tools, carts, trees and even turf, for military purposes, usually on mere promise of payment. People living in the suburbs of garrisoned towns were liable to have their houses burned to clear an area around the fortifications. There was always the danger that soldiers stationed in the district would begin to loot, from desperation or sheer greed: it was estimated that the depredations of 700 troopers sent to protect Worcester during the campaign of 1643 cost the county more than the food bill for the entire royal army of 20,000 men stationed in it.

What these burdens could mean is illustrated by the petition of a man who lived near Ludlow, delivered in 1644. He had lost his three horses in succession and then had his spade taken to dig fortifications, leaving him with no means of growing crops, a family to support, the local rate to pay and a soldier to feed and accommodate. He had been ruined, before the war had even come near him.[8]

When the war did come, its consequences could be horrific. Certain areas were deliberately devastated to destroy the resources of the party which possessed them, the corn burned and the cattle driven off. A town taken by storm was, by tradition, sacked by the victors. This process enabled armies to survive without pay, and inspired their men to rush fortifications. Some carried home enough cloth to keep their families warm for years. Sometimes, in the course of an assault, parts of a town would be set on fire: in this way half of Bridgwater went up. Lancaster was burned by a departing army which had failed to capture its castle, as an act of anger and frustration. The numerous long sieges of the war imposed a different sort of suffering upon townspeople. Those of Carlisle were allegedly reduced to eating rats and dogs, and after its eventual surrender the occupying force found it 'the very model of misery and desolation, as sword, famine and plague left it'.[9]

For villagers, the worst experience was to be in a borderland between zones of occupation, paying money to both sides and being fought over and looted by their soldiers. In 1643 the aged earl of Middlesex, living in parliament's territory, received this note from the agent on his Gloucestershire estates:

> I have lent money to both sides. Been plundered by both sides. Been imprisoned by both sides. A mad world.[10]

From the beginning, country people sometimes violently resisted pillaging troops. As the war went on, garrisons multiplied, local warfare intensified, and rural associations for mutual protection were formed in many districts, with sentries, alarm signals and mass risings of the inhabitants. These 'Clubmen' could field thousands, and were powerful enough to blockade fortresses, but as their name suggests neither their equipment nor their training were very impressive. As soon as a regular army entered their area they were doomed, and in every case these groups ended up either surrendering or being destroyed.

Civilians who manufactured clothing or weapons for the war may have made a personal profit from it, but it is doubtful whether many such contractors were properly paid. Certainly none of them made fortunes. In the few areas hardly touched by the fighting, such as East Anglia, daily life would have gone on as before, save for taxation, conscription, reduced trade and fear of attack, but this was a dreary enough burden. There was, in addition, a less tangible strain in very many places: the experience of being forbidden to pay rents to the accustomed landlord or to listen to the familiar parson, because these individuals had been considered enemies by the party dominating the area.

Tenants could find one group of soldiers and civilian commissioners demanding their taxes or rates and another taking their rents, while their landlord threatened them with eviction for non-payment. As some gentry, attempting to stay neutral, were declared opponents by both sides, a change in the military situation did not always bring relief. If the great majority of the English and Welsh were reluctant to let the war begin, then they were desperate to see it end.

All this suffering was inflicted upon a country which had probably been the most peaceful in Europe, and had for seventy years enjoyed the longest period of internal stability in its history. For three generations the number of treason trials and executions had steadily declined, and the notion of a national code of laws been ever more firmly accepted. Most villages experienced from two to four cases of violent crime in a century. Travellers remarked upon the safety of the roads, and the rich built their houses without defences. To such a society, the Civil War was not a natural lapse into violence but a nightmare inconceivable until it occurred.

So what, then, was the course of this conflict? In 1642, as described, the partisans used their own resources against each other, and the result was indecisive. In 1643 they began to squeeze money out of the general public, but despite savage fighting, in which the royalists conquered the western counties, final victory was still not achieved. In 1644 more taxation, and conscription, were imposed, and both parties brought in allies: parliament bought an army from the Scots and Charles recalled the royal army from Ireland. After a desperate struggle the royalists lost most of the North, but hung on to the rest of their territory.

By early 1645, neither side had any fresh resources upon which to call, and some regions were showing signs of exhaustion. A royalist commander quartered in Gloucestershire complained to his general that the towns were falling into ruin and their shops closed. He was not worried about the local people but about supplying his men.[11] A few months later, parliament's Scottish allies in the Midlands sent the following chilling message to London: 'We are called to march, march, march, that a plentiful country is still before us, but we find nothing by the way but solitude'.[12]

To the task of forcing materials from an unwilling population, both parties had now sacrificed much of the traditional social order. Parliament filled up its local committees and its officer corps with people from outside the pre-war ruling elite, picked for their efficiency. The king put his territory under military men with no previous connection with the area each governed, to avoid any inconvenient sympathy of ruler for ruled. Over half of his field officers, the highest-ranking men in his armies, came from below the rank of gentry. In June 1645 the royalist earl of Berkshire, a privy councillor, wrote to a friend that the soldiers on both sides would enrich themselves by plundering noblemen's estates. He added, 'Nobody can tell what we have been fighting about all this while'.[13]

5.7. A petition detailing
losses to the army

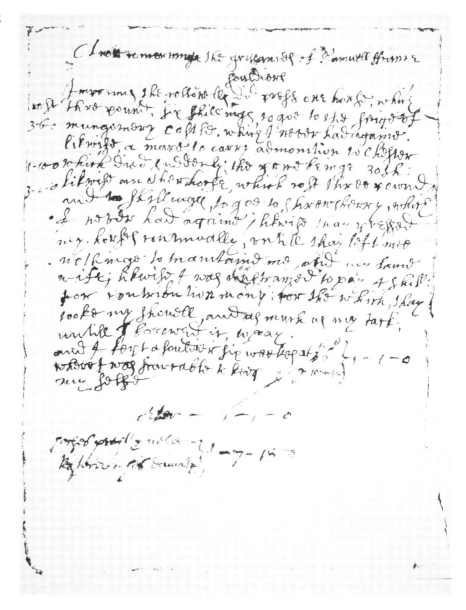

In fact, a decisive victory was at last possible, as neither side *had*
fresh reserves to fall back upon. The king seemed likely to win it, as he
swept across the Midlands. But at Naseby, with fatal over-confidence,
his army charged uphill into a bigger force without waiting for the
regiments marching to join it, and was destroyed. This need not have
meant the end, for Charles retreated into the heart of his territory and
demanded the men and money for a new army. But the local people,

led by their gentry, refused: they wanted an end to the war more than anything else, and Charles now lacked soldiers to compel them to support it. Thus the royalist war effort was now paralysed and parliament's troops able to reduce the king's fortresses one by one. In one sense Charles I lost the Civil War because he lost some battles. In another, it was because the community, which had not started the war, was eventually able to stop it.

One more question must be answered: could it happen again? If it was not, after all, the result of some fundamental upheaval in society, but of a terrible mistake by society's rulers, the answer may be yes. Let us suppose that a government was elected in Britain with a tiny overall majority of seats, and proceeded to implement a fundamental change either in the distribution of private property or in our system of national defence. Let us suppose that the opposition parties then called upon the public, and the armed forces, to resist this change, on the grounds that only a minority of the population had actually voted for this ministry. Most probably, a few partisans would respond upon each side, and fighting would begin, and then escalate. Ultimately, the remarkable peace of this country for over two centuries has depended upon a mixture of good luck and self-restraint. This is not, perhaps, a comforting conclusion.

Further reading

Robert Ashton, *The English Civil War* (London, 1978); John Morrill, *The Revolt of the Provinces* (London, 1980); John Morrill (ed.), *Reactions to the English Civil War* (Basingstoke, 1982); Ronald Hutton, *The Royalist War Effort, 1642–1646* (London, 1982); P.R. Newman, *Atlas of the English Civil War* (London, 1985).

CHAPTER SIX

Restoration and the Rise of Party

Mark Goldie

The parliamentarian gentry who had gone to war against Charles I in the 1640s eagerly restored his son Charles II to the throne in 1660. They were weary and frightened men. They had set out to rescue a Protestant nation from 'popery and arbitrary power', but the Civil War had quite unexpectedly opened a Pandora's Box of disasters for the governing elite. King-killing, republican experiments, Leveller questioning of the social order, the anarchism of new-fangled religious sects, and the petty dictatorship of upstart colonels – all these deeply threatened the gentry's traditional authority. In abject retreat, the old parliamentarians repudiated the extremists they had spawned, made their peace with the Cavaliers, and in a general election in 1661 were swept aside on a tide of royalist reaction.

The puritan cry of 'Godly Reformation' now provoked suspicion and jaundice. As the Speaker of the House of Commons declared, 'We are sick of Reformation'. To the old fear of popish absolutism from above was now added the new fear of 'Godly' fanaticism from below.[1] These two fears were to dominate the minds of the English governing classes for generations to come. Their anxieties long outlasted the realities of these threats, for by the end of the seventeenth century the nobility and gentry had entrenched themselves with remarkable success, and ensured that neither Rome nor the New Jerusalem would be built in England. But the monolithic stability of the governing elite that was to last throughout the eighteenth century and beyond was not easily won.[2] The era we call Restoration England – the long reign of Charles II from 1660 to 1685, and the brief reign of his Roman Catholic brother James II until 1688 – was marked by the road to absolutism, by republican plots, by fears of renewed civil war, and by a political crisis which gave birth to two political parties known as Tory and Whig. The era culminated in the second revolution of the

century, traditionally known as the Glorious Revolution, when, in the
winter of 1688–9, for the last time in English history, a king was
deposed. The Catholic James fled and gave way to the Protestant
Dutchman William of Orange. We can best understand these events
by watching the shifting tides of those two deeply embedded anxieties,
the fears of the popery of Rome and the fanaticism of the puritans.

The fear of Rome was in abeyance in Charles II's early years. The
campaign against the alleged popery of his father's court and his
father's bishops had produced the reality of lunatic extremists bent on
destroying everything in the name of Reformation. Samuel Butler's
Hudibras, the anti-puritan poem which the king and the Cavaliers
knew by heart, has it that the puritans

> Call Fire, and Sword, and Desolation,
> A Godly thorough Reformation.[3]

It is not surprising that the gentry now felt that the power of the king
in the state and of bishops in the church were essential pillars of their
own social and political authority in the counties. The venerable
Ancient Constitution was reconstructed wholesale. In the wake of the
innovative constitutional schemes of the Interregnum, the medieval
parliamentary electoral system was restored, and left untouched to
become increasingly ramshackle and unrepresentative.[4] The House of
Lords, which had been abolished in 1649 along with the monarchy,
assumed its old constitutional role: it continued to be as important a
part of parliament as the Commons. The bishops and the Book of
Common Prayer had been abolished too; now the old Church of
England returned, still financed by the medieval tithes, still exerting
discipline over morals and worship in the ecclesiastical courts, and its
parsons gradually becoming the tame adjuncts of the squires.[5]
Crucially, county government was restored to the hands of the all-
powerful Justices of the Peace, and not until Victorian times did
modern, elective, and bureaucratic local authorities take their place.
The office of JP was, for the county elite, the key to their status and
influence.[6]

So far as the king's authority was concerned, the memory of puritan
upheaval made the gentry remarkably obsequious. It is true that some
of the king's earlier powers were not restored. Neither the prerogative
courts, such as Star Chamber, nor the feudal courts, such as the Court
of Wards, were revived. But the overwhelmingly royalist parliament
which met in 1661, known as the Cavalier Parliament, handed back to
the crown what the Long Parliament of the 1640s had taken away:
control over the military, and over the appointment of the officers of
state. Most importantly, in 1664 they repealed, at the king's request,

the Triennial Act of 1641, which had required regular parliaments. The king was thereby handed the constitutional trump card, and he played it with skill. He kept the Cavalier Parliament in being for eighteen years, because it was generally so acquiescent. When, on the other hand, he was confronted in 1681 by a recalcitrant parliament, he peremptorily dissolved it after only one week's sitting. He then did without parliament altogether for the remainder of his life. His brother James held only one parliament, in the opening months of his reign, and dismissed it when it would not allow him to appoint Catholics to public office.[7]

The remarkable lack of conditions placed upon the crown at the Restoration was a foundation upon which Charles and James were able to build in later years. By the 1680s the king could financially afford to do without parliament, a rare feat for a Stuart monarch. This was not so much because of handouts from the French king, Louis XIV, as used to be thought, but because reforms at the Treasury, and a healthy economy, combined to produce high tax revenues, particularly from the customs and excise. The government even managed to abolish the tax farm system, by which private contractors took their cut from the revenues, a centralising reform Louis XIV could not achieve. Moreover, both Charles and James began to exercise wider powers. Judges were appointed and dismissed to secure favourable decisions in the courts. Unco-operative JPs were sacked in increasingly extensive purges of the county and borough magistracies. The royal charters of scores of boroughs were rewritten, in a massive administrative operation designed to secure royal authority in town government.[8]

Perhaps the most important long-term development was the increasing manipulation of parliament through the patronage system. The power of appointment to nearly all offices lay with the crown, and by dangling court sinecures in front of MPs, or by threatening to cut off their existing posts, a pliable court interest could be built up in the House of Commons. For many gentlemen, public office, a post perhaps as an excise commissioner, or in the Navy Office, was a matter of necessary income, as well as of honour. The holders of these posts came to be called 'placemen', and their systematic use began with the earl of Danby, who was Charles II's chief minister in the 1670s. There is a case for calling Danby the first prime minister, since his high office, and his value to the king, depended primarily on his ability to secure a working majority in the Commons. When that majority crumbled, the king allowed him to fall.[9] The crown, therefore, sought not only to bypass parliament, but also to tame it. This was an altogether more far-reaching development. Constitutional ideals dictated that parliament should consist of independent and incorruptible members whose job was to legislate in the public interest, and not in the private interest of courtiers and men of power. But constitutional practice was otherwise, and in spite of attempts to turf the placemen out of parliament, the British constitution has never satisfactorily restrained the power of the executive over the legislature. In the eighteenth century the manipulation of the patronage system was brought to a high art. The chief constitutional legacy of the Restoration, therefore, was the centralising of the patronage system in the hands of the state. The Revolution of 1689 merely accelerated the process, so that, in this light, both king *and* parliament were the losers after 1689, and the winners were whichever party amongst the aristocratic elite got its hands on the patronage system.

But this is to anticipate, because before the Revolution the chief beneficiary of a complaisant parliament was the king. By the 1680s England was on a path towards absolutism. The Civil War, as a project for decisively restraining the king's prerogatives – his personal constitutional powers – had been a failure.[10] The Cavalier gentry, in retreat from the puritan catastrophe, were ready to help the king into the absolutist saddle. At no other time did such a large proportion of the governing classes believe in the divine right of kings, and the inviolable duty of obedience. This was the time of the cult of Charles I, king and martyr, the symbol of patriarchal kingship and Anglican piety. Churchmen regularly preached on the text of Romans 13: 'the powers that be are ordained of God ... and they that resist shall receive to themselves damnation'. The Cavalier Parliament enacted a new oath, required of all office-holders, which declared 'that it is not lawful upon any pretence whatsoever to take arms against the King'. They narrowly failed to get a majority to enact yet another oath to promise not to 'endeavour any alteration in the government in church or state'.[11]

Behind this passionate royalism there was, however, a crucial assumption – that the king would be sensible enough to maintain a partnership with them, the natural governors, and with their cherished Church of England. When that partnership flourished, as it did for much of Charles' reign, it left them a free hand to seek vengeance upon their puritan enemies. The statutes of the 1660s purged the church, the borough corporations and the universities. By the Act of Uniformity of 1662 nearly 2000 parish ministers were driven from their parishes, their consciences unable to accept the rituals and the episcopal authority they had so recently helped to destroy. The tradition of Protestant Nonconformity, or Dissent, dates from this time, a tradition of Presbyterians, Congregationalists, Baptists and Quakers, seeking some tolerance within English society. They were not legally to be allowed to worship openly until the Toleration Act of

1689, and they were formally excluded from public office until 1828. In the Restoration era, militant bishops and Cavalier gentlemen had high hopes of destroying them altogether. Many Quakers died in jail, and the famous devotional writers John Bunyan, a Baptist, and Richard Baxter, a Presbyterian, were jailed. This mood of Anglican exclusiveness – the notion that only Anglican churchmen could loyally support the crown, the belief that puritan 'fanatics' and 'republicans' were itching to overthrow monarchy and the social order – was the spirit which I have so far called Cavalier, but it soon acquired the name of Tory. In time its harsher edges became moderated, but for two centuries the Tory party was to consider itself essentially the party of church, king and squire.

The emergence of the Tory tradition is, however, by no means the whole story of Restoration England. For in the 1670s that other anxiety, about popish kingship, came to the surface again. It soon changed the face of politics, and polarised the governing classes. There was a simple reason for this. It became public knowledge that the heir to the throne, James, duke of York, had converted to Catholicism. The prospect of a Catholic monarch instantly brought to English minds the memory of the burning of Protestants in Smithfield in the reign of the previous Catholic monarch, Mary I (1553–8), famously depicted in John Foxe's *Book of Martyrs*. Since the time that Queen Elizabeth had triumphed over the Armada, and James I had escaped assassination in the Gunpowder Plot, Protestants had believed England to be chosen by Providence to be the flagship of 'true religion' in a world of Catholic darkness. The duty of a Protestant monarch was to be vigilant against the machinations of the Roman Antichrist. A Catholic king was incompatible with England and the Reformation.

In 1678 a match was put to the tinder-box of apprehension. A man called Titus Oates disclosed a plot to assassinate Charles and bring England forcibly back to the bosom of the Roman Church. This Popish Plot was a total fabrication, but two events ensured that it was believed. The first was that the magistrate appointed to investigate the plot allegations was found murdered on Primrose Hill in north London, a crime never yet solved, but immediately attributed to the papists. The second was that a search of the apartment of the duke of York's secretary, who was a Catholic priest, turned up some correspondence with Paris and Rome which could be read in an incriminating way, and which led to the secretary's execution for treason. For many months a frenzied pursuit of Catholics took place, the last severe persecution of Catholicism, in which some twenty priests were executed, the final victims in the tally of the English Catholic martyrs.[12]

One man, the earl of Shaftesbury, was especially keen that papist

S.ʳ William Waller burning Popiſh books, Images, and Reliques

Dʳ Oates diſcovereth y̆ Plot to y̆ King and Councell.

plotters be hunted down, for he saw this as a device to close in upon the duke of York himself.[13] In 1679 he proposed in parliament that James be excluded from the succession on the ground that his Catholicism was incompatible with a Protestant constitution. The crisis which ensued shows with great clarity the dynamic of the gentry's two anxieties. They all feared popish despotism and puritan subversion. What now divided them into two parties was a judgement about which was the most imminent and pressing threat. Those who feared popery more than puritan zealotry followed Shaftesbury and came to be called Whigs. They felt that the prerogative power of the popishly inclined Stuarts should be permanently limited, and also believed that toleration should be granted to Protestant Nonconformists in order to create a broad Protestant solidarity against the Romish threat. Those, on the other hand, who feared puritan fanaticism more

6.1. Two playing cards attributed to Frances Barlow, depicting the Popish Plot

than a Catholic king came to be called Tories. They thought that James should be allowed to succeed Charles. They believed James would not risk an ambitious Catholic policy; they also thought that to exclude him by law was dangerously radical and tantamount to elective monarchy and a right of deposition. They believed, correctly, that Charles was not prepared to sacrifice his brother and the sacred inheritance of the House of Stuart. And lastly they knew that their old leader, Danby, had taken the precaution of marrying the next heir but one, James's Protestant daughter Mary, to the impeccably Protestant Dutch prince, William of Orange. For these reasons the Tories stood by Charles and his brother. A scene in the House of Commons summed up the matter. An angry Whig shouted 'I am not for popery'; a Tory replied 'Nor I for presbytery': they came to blows.[14]

6.2. A pope-burning procession in 1680

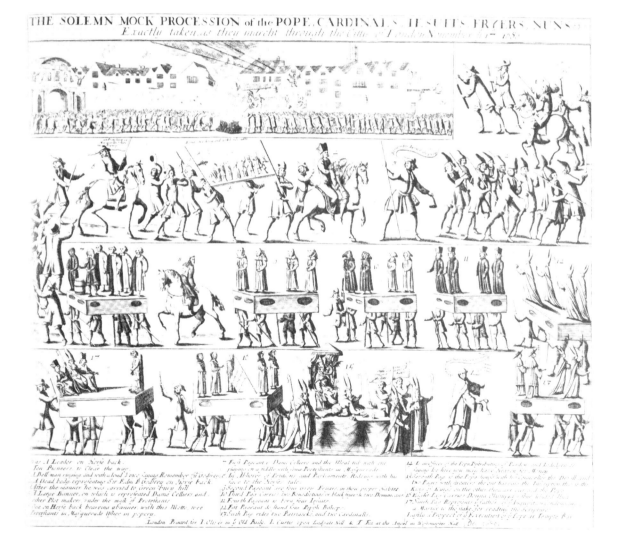

The Whigs' proposal to exclude James was made three times in three successive parliaments, and achieved a majority in the Commons. Three times the king thwarted it, either by using his prerogative power of dissolution, or by his influence over the House of Lords. For many months the situation was extremely volatile, and when Charles fell seriously ill there were fears of another civil war. There was intense electioneering, a massive propaganda war, bitter gentry factionalism in the counties, vigorous attempts to organise MPs into one lobby or another, and the drumming up of rival demonstrations in the streets. In short, the Exclusion Crisis gave birth to something like a party political system.

The outcome was total success for the king and the Tories. The last Exclusion Parliament, which Charles summoned to Oxford to escape London's Whig mobs, was dismissed after a week. The Whigs were taken completely by surprise, and they dared not rebel. The king had the whiphand over parliament, but it was as much a victory for the Tories as for him, since Charles was only able to call the Whigs' bluff because there had occurred a remarkable shift in public opinion towards the Tory and court point of view. At the outset of the crisis, with the Popish Plot revelations a fresh shock, middle-of-the-road opinion had swung towards the Whigs. But as the crisis wore on, Shaftesbury's Whigs overplayed their hand. Knowing that anti-popish passion was what kept them afloat, they began to accuse more and more respectable Protestant courtiers and Anglican bishops of complicity in the Popish Plot, or at least of fatal indifference to the popish threat. This political witch-hunt, under the guise of rooting out popery in high places, soon reminded the political nation of the atmosphere of the 1640s, when puritan zealots had set about destroying the court and the church in the name of Protestant purity. The cry of 'No Popery' again came to look like a cover for a revolutionary republican plot. The fear of puritan fanaticism blossomed once more, and the tide turned towards the Tories. The Tories offered themselves as a middle way between two extremes, and they in turn accused Whigs and Dissenters of being hand-in-glove with the papists, since both types of extremists aimed to destroy the king and the church. The Whig pope-burning carnivals were now matched by Tory mobs burning effigies of Cromwell and 'Jack Presbyter', the black-gowned symbol of puritan fanaticism. The Tory's leading propagandist, Sir Roger L'Estrange, produced a powerful cartoon called *The Committee*, in which representatives of the puritan sects, from a Presbyterian through to a naked promiscuous 'Adamite', meet to plot revolution; in the background the pope of Rome is seen to agree with them on the downfall of England's institutions.

In Charles II's last years the Tories were triumphant. The king gave

6.3. A Wiltshire playing
card depicting the Rye
House Plot

them a free hand to purge and persecute Whigs and Dissenters, and
they readily used prerogative powers to do so. Shaftesbury fled to
Holland in the wake of a treason charge brought against him. A
handful of Whigs were driven to plot a *coup d'état*, the Rye House
Plot of 1683, which aimed to assassinate Charles on his way from
Newmarket races. The plot was uncovered, and the Tories had their
proof that the Whigs were revolutionary terrorists. The radical
political theorist Algernon Sidney was executed, and the philosopher
John Locke fled to Holland. Hence it was that, despite the anti-popery
tradition, the Catholic James successfully came to the throne in 1685.
In the summer of that year his Tory friends in parliament
unswervingly supported him in defeating the final fling of the old Civil
War puritan radicals. This was the rebellion of the duke of
Monmouth, the charismatic, Protestant and illegitimate son of Charles

II. His impromptu army of West Country craftsmen and shopkeepers was either cut down on the battlefield of Sedgemoor, or strung up by Judge Jeffrey's Bloody Assize. Monmouth himself was executed.[15]

We come now to the final act in the Restoration drama, the last turn of the tide of the gentry's anxieties. In 1685 the Tories had the country in a vice-like grip, and the Stuart crown was at its most powerful. The partnership was unstoppable, and the Tories were totally confident that James would not dare risk anything more than practising his Catholicism in his private chapel. They were in for a brutal shock. James was determined to transform the sad circumstances of English Catholicism. He had no intention of renewing the fires of Smithfield, but he wished to promote Catholics in public life and to encourage conversions. When the Tories and churchmen refused to compromise on the Anglican monopoly of public office, James decided to break the vital partnership. In the spring of 1686 he set out on the path which led to his downfall. James has been described as an 'old man in a hurry'. With great energy he set about his campaign, appointing Catholics to positions in government, the army and the universities. By 1688 nearly one-third of the Privy Council were Catholics, and one-fifth of the JPs. Catholic chapels and schools were opened. Catholic books poured from government presses, with the convert Poet Laureate John Dryden contributing his poem *The Hind and the Panther* to the propaganda effort.

James was, however, well aware that a purely Catholic regime was too narrow a power base, since only about one per cent of the population was Catholic. So he tried to forge a broad alliance of all the Tories' enemies. A number of Whigs, despite their old antipathy to James and Catholicism, were attracted by the opportunity to strike back at the Tories — and few knew that William of Orange was planning to offer them a better solution to their problems. The Nonconformists, similarly, were in a desperate condition, and took advantage of James's offer of a general toleration. In 1687, James issued his Declaration of Indulgence, by which he suspended the statutes which gave the monopoly of worship to Anglicanism. (His brother Charles had issued a similar Declaration in 1672, but had soon been forced to withdraw it by the Cavalier Parliament.[16]) James appointed a considerable number of Nonconformists and Whigs as JPs and Privy Councillors. By the summer of 1688, in massive purges of the county magistracies, the king had swept from office almost the entire Anglican gentry elite, and when he ran out of Catholic gentry to appoint in their place he turned to Presbyterians, Baptists and even Quakers and Cromwellian colonels. Sir Thomas Strickland of Westmorland, his family typical of the rural enclaves of Catholicism which were excluded from public life between Elizabeth's and

Victoria's time, suddenly found himself in the Privy Council. Ambrose Barnes, a Nonconformist merchant of Newcastle, who had been an alderman under Cromwell, but firmly excluded ever since, was an alderman once more.

The horror and anger all this aroused in the Tory gentry knew no bounds. The pulpits thundered with anti-popery sermons, and the gentry and bishops engaged in civil disobedience where they could. Whig aristocrats meanwhile – those who were not prepared to be wooed by James – engaged in secret negotiations with the Dutch Prince William. James II had managed a remarkable feat: he had provoked both of the two great fears. His was, ironically, a regime of papists *and* puritans, and he seemed like a Charles I and a Cromwell rolled into one. The two final straws came in the summer of 1688. James put the archbishop of Canterbury and six other bishops into the Tower of London on a charge of sedition. His wife, meanwhile, unexpectedly produced a son and heir, thus displacing his Protestant daughters, and raising the spectre of an indefinite Catholic monarchy. Against this background William, whose sole concern was to turn the

6.4. The landing of William of Orange

IV. His R.H. the Prince of Orange going for England.
Novemb. 2. 1688.

IV. Syn K.H. vertrekt naar Engeland,
Den 11 Nov. 1688.

IV.

resources of England against the Catholic expansionism of Louis xiv of France, decided to take an astonishing gamble. He left Holland unprotected, sailed with an army, borne along (it was said) by a Protestant wind, and landed at Torbay in Devon. For the last time England was successfully invaded. William did not, however, need to fight any battles, since the English governing classes, the army officers and the churchmen deserted James wholesale. On the verge of mental breakdown, James fled to France with his newborn son, to begin the long history of forlorn Jacobite hopes of recapturing the throne. His Protestant daughter and son-in-law were raised to the throne as William iii and Mary ii.

The Whigs, despite the earlier failure of the Exclusion plan, had now got their way, and their fundamental principle was built into the Act of Settlement of 1701, by which England's monarchy became, and has since remained, Protestant by law.[17] It is often said that the Tories and the churchmen were turncoats in 1688, ditching their pious beliefs in divine right kingship and non-resistance when their own position came under threat from James. It is true they had to compromise when William and Mary were crowned, but they had always believed that their first duty, and that of their monarch, was to uphold the 'true religion', as they saw it, and the social order which they thought to be a reflection of God's divine order. By 1700 they were becoming reconciled to the end of royal absolutism, and to a partial tolerance of the Nonconformists. The Whigs compromised too; they dissociated themselves from constitutional extremism, and made sure that republican idealism played no part in this revolution. They left the Church of England intact, giving the Nonconformists only minimal tolerance. And with Catholic monarchy removed, the Catholics were left in peace. After 1688 people no longer died for their religion.

Between 1660 and 1700 the nobility and gentry had achieved a considerable solidarity, and had steered themselves through a dangerous channel between the rocks of popish and puritan subversion. On the other hand, their division about how best to pilot the ship of state had given rise to the two political traditions of Tory and Whig, two divergent and powerful conceptions of the proper relationship between Protestantism and the social order, which were to shape English party politics for centuries to come. For it was not until the beginning of the present century that the language of class finally replaced the language of religion as the chief way in which English people orientated themselves to their political life.[18]

Further reading

P. Jenkins, *The Making of a Ruling Class: The Glamorgan Gentry 1640–1790* (Cambridge, 1983); J.R. Jones, *The Revolution of 1688 in England* (London, 1972); J.R. Jones (ed.), *The Restored Monarchy 1660–88* (London, 1979); J.P. Kenyon, *The Popish Plot* (London, 1972); J. Miller, *Popery and Politics in England 1660–88* (Cambridge, 1973); J.H. Plumb, *The Growth of Political Stability in England 1675–1725* (London, 1967); J.R. Western, *Monarchy and Revolution: The English State in the 1680s* (London, 1972).

Revolution to Robinocracy

William Speck

This chapter looks at the effects of the Revolution of 1688 on the political life of Britain. It traces the way in which the constitutional problems of the seventeenth century were gradually resolved during the reigns of William III, Queen Anne and George I, and how this made possible the political stability presided over by Sir Robert Walpole from 1720 to 1742. Walpole's grip on the country was so firm that his ministry became known as the Robinocracy, after his first name. Prime Minister Robin, a bluff, blunt, shrewd and ambitious Norfolk squire, seemed to personify his own stable regime in his portly, overweight figure.

His achievement was the more remarkable coming so soon after the turbulence of the Stuart era, which had experienced two civil wars, the execution of Charles I, a short-lived republic, a shaky Restoration settlement, and the Revolution of 1688. By contrast, under the early Hanoverians a political system emerged strong enough to withstand the challenges posed by two Jacobite rebellions, the American and French revolutions and the social and economic disruptions caused by a population explosion and the onset of industrialisation.

This transition from what has been called 'the Century of Revolution' to what is now generally regarded as the classic era of stability was a complex process. Two crucial developments promoted its growth. One was the gradual cooling of issues which had kept the political temperature at boiling point under the Stuarts. The other was the evolution of a smoother working relationship between the crown and parliament. Three political issues split the nation between the Revolution of 1688 and the accession of the House of Hanover. These were: the succession to the throne; the relationship between the Church of England and other religious denominations; and Britain's role in Europe.

The issues of the succession and religion were personified in King James II, as hereditary successor to his brother Charles II and as a zealous convert to Catholicism. The Tory Party defended his right to succeed on the grounds that kings ruled by divine, indefeasible, hereditary succession. Tories held kings to be accountable to God alone, and not to their subjects, and insisted that resistance to the Lord's anointed was sinful. Even if he began to act tyrannically, all that the subject could do was to practise passive obedience and non-resistance. The Whig Party maintained that kings were responsible to their subjects, who had the right to resist an arbitrary monarch. They also claimed that James ruled arbitrarily, by dispensing with parliament, issuing edicts and raising an army to cow his people into submission.

The king's actions alienated a majority in both England and Scotland. Consequently, when William of Orange invaded in November 1688, James had only his army to defend him against the invader. The vast majority of his subjects simply stood on the sidelines, waiting to see the outcome of the contest. Although James's

7.1. The arrival of William III in London

forces outnumbered William's by two to one, a conspiracy among his own officers led to a number of key desertions at the critical moment. Their treachery unnerved the king, who decided to flee rather than to fight. Thus the Revolution was at least bloodless, even if it was not altogether glorious.

James's flight to France forced political leaders in all his kingdoms to decide where their loyalties lay. Enough English politicians decided in favour of the succession of William and Mary to avoid armed conflict. While a majority of Scottish parliamentarians agreed on the same solution, there were sufficient counter-revolutionaries in Scotland to plunge that country into a minor civil war. In Ireland those Catholics placed in authority by James remained loyal to him when he fled, necessitating the post-revolutionary conquest of that kingdom by the adherents of William of Orange.

In settling the crown on James's daughter and her Dutch husband, the English parliament overlooked not only James himself but his infant son, James Francis Edward, and thus made a major breach in the hereditary succession. This seemed to mark the triumph of the Whig view. Yet the transition from divine right to parliamentary monarchy did not come about overnight in 1689. Tories obstinately clung to their theory of hereditary succession despite the facts.

James II's flight could be explained as abdication, or a conquest, and even explained away as divine disapproval on an errant monarch. Moreover, many refused to accept that James Edward was his son, finding comfort in the fantastic notion that the baby had been smuggled into the queen's bedchamber in a warming pan. When Anne, James's younger daughter, succeeded to the throne in 1702, a year after her father's death, there was even a revival of the divine right theory in some Tory circles. Not until the accession of George I in 1714 set aside some fifty claimants closer to the trunk of the Stuart family tree did it become quite impossible for Tories to reconcile the facts with their traditional doctrines. Some preferred to uphold the hereditary principle, and to become Jacobites, as adherents of James's son were styled. Most however resigned themselves to the Protestant succession in the House of Hanover, few joining in the Jacobite rebellions of 1715 or 1745.[1]

In Scotland the split over the succession was far more clear cut. Where there was some ambiguity among English politicians about what occurred in 1689, the Scottish Whigs made no bones of the fact that they had deposed James VII, while Tories were unequivocally Jacobite north of the border. The result was that the succession had to be fought for at Killiecrankie and Dunkeld in 1689, Sheriffmuir in 1715 and Prestonpans, Falkirk and Culloden during the 'Forty-five.

It was because the Scottish parliament threatened to break with the

Hanoverian succession during Anne's reign that the English government took alarm and negotiated a Union in 1707. Most Scots probably regarded the Union as a shot-gun marriage, brought about by a crude mixture of bribery and threats. A Scottish economic miracle, confidently predicted by some of its advocates, including Daniel Defoe, failed to materialise in the years immediately after its passage, though by mid-century the lowlands at least were beginning to benefit from incorporation in the economy of the British empire. Prosperity fostered the development of political stability in Scotland. Despite the spectacular success of Scottish Jacobites in the 'Forty-five they in fact had far less support then, even in the highlands, than they had commanded during the 'Fifteen.

Where the northern kingdom, at least in theory, enjoyed equal status with England in the Union of Great Britain, the conquest of Ireland completed the process whereby that country was reduced to little more than a British colony. James II sailed from France to take possession of his Irish kingdom in 1689, forcing William to lead an expedition to wrest it from him the following year. In 1690 the two contenders for the crown of Ireland faced each other across the river Boyne. William's victory in the subsequent battle, followed by James's second flight to France, led to the collapse of Irish resistance in 1691. Thereafter the Roman Catholics were excluded from political power

7.2. William III at the Battle of the Boyne

and subordinated to the Protestant minority.

In none of the three kingdoms were religious problems confined to a straightforward clash between Catholics and Protestants. On the contrary, they all witnessed a triangular conflict between an established Protestant Church on the one hand, and dissenters from it, Protestant as well as Catholic, on the other. The Anglican Church of Ireland was just as hostile to the Ulster Presbyterians as it was to the Irish Catholics. The Presbyterian Church of Scotland was if possible more opposed to bishops than it was to Catholics, and took advantage of the Revolution to abolish bishoprics, thus ensuring that Scottish Episcopalians became the most zealous Jacobites in Britain. The Church of England had been intolerant of Nonconformists as well as of Roman Catholics throughout the reign of Charles II, when such sects as Presbyterians, Baptists and Quakers had all suffered persecution.

After the Revolution, however, the Convention Parliament passed the Toleration Act in 1689, which allowed non-Catholics who believed in the Trinity to worship separately from the Church of England without molestation. Although this was the outcome of the alliance between Anglicans and Dissenters brought about by James II's pro-Catholic policy, it did not inaugurate a period of mutual goodwill between them. Instead relations between them remained poor, since the Act led to the secession from the Church of England of many former Anglicans, who chose to worship in the now tolerated chapels of its rivals, or even to refrain from attending church at all. This alarmed many Anglican ministers, who saw their position in society being threatened by the rise of dissent. They expressed their alarm with the cry 'The Church in danger'.

Tories supported the claims of the Church of England that it was in danger from these trends. They joined in demands that Convocation should convene to combat the ill effects of the Toleration Act, which went beyond the rise of dissent to an increase in deism, religious indifference and even outright atheism.[2]

The consequent controversies reached their height in the last four years of Queen Anne's reign. During that Indian summer of Stuart Toryism from 1710 to 1714 the Nonconformists suffered renewed persecution. Their chapels were ransacked by rioting mobs in London and the provinces. Statutes were passed in parliament restricting their civil liberties, including their right to educate their children in their own schools.[3]

When the Whigs came into their own on the accession of George I, the ousted Tories feared that they would retaliate by launching a counter-attack upon the Church of England. Certainly they suppressed Convocation, which did not meet again until the nineteenth century.

They also repealed the controversial Acts passed since 1710. But the worst Tory fears were not realised. Successive Whig governments refused to remove the remaining disabilities from Dissenters for the rest of the eighteenth century. The result was a compromise on the religious issues which had threatened to tear society apart under the Stuarts. The volcano might not have become extinct after its last major eruption in Anne's reign but, apart from occasional rumblings, it lay dormant under the early Hanoverians. This too contributed much to the political stability over which Walpole presided.

The question of involvement in European conflict also became less divisive under the first two Georges than it had been under William and Anne. From 1689 to 1713 Britain became involved in two major wars against France. As far as possible Walpole kept the country at peace.

During the wars against France the Whigs had earned a reputation as a war party, while the Tories projected themselves as the party of peace. The two parties acquired their images as hawks and doves during the wars because of their differing attitudes towards the role Britain should play in Europe. Apart from a brief interlude under Oliver Cromwell, the country had played a minor part in European affairs during the seventeenth century. But Cromwell had shown the potential for acquiring major power status if British resources were geared to war. Neither Charles II nor James II had wished to continue the Cromwellian tradition, and during their reigns Britain appeared to be one of the many satellites of France. It was precisely to get her out of the French orbit that William of Orange invaded in 1688. After the Revolution, British assets were fully committed to conflict with the French king, Louis XIV.

The Whigs enthusiastically accepted this dramatic change of policy, seeing Louis XIV as a threat to Protestantism and Liberty throughout Europe. To them the wars were one long war of the British succession, since Louis backed James II in the first and his son in the second. Tories, however, adjusted badly to the new continental development. Initially they would have preferred Britain to play a minor role in Europe, preferably as a sea power rather than as a major contributor to the military effort. As the wars dragged on, especially the second, the War of the Spanish Succession, they came to demand withdrawal from them. These differing attitudes sprang partly from the effects of the burden of supporting great power status. William's war cost roughly £5,000,000 a year and Anne's more like £7,000,000. These were unprecedented sums: James II's total expenditure had been around £2,000,000 per annum. To help raise these amounts required the introduction of a regular direct tax on income from land for the first time since the days of Cromwell. Fixed at a wartime rate of four shillings in the pound, this was in theory a 20 per cent income tax on rents. Although in practice the burden was rarely as heavy as that, it did give rise to complaints that landlords were being bled white to pay for the war effort. Meanwhile the government anticipated the yield of the land tax and other revenues by borrowing to finance the wars. This system of public credit created a national debt and a whole financial machinery to service it, at the centre of which was the Bank of England, established in 1694. To the complaints of landowners were added accusations that the state's creditors were profiting from the wars.

The Tory Party took up these claims. It identified itself with landowners whose incomes were allegedly being squeezed by war taxation, and the Whigs with the monied interest, as they called those involved in public credit. They even went so far as to accuse the Whigs of a conspiracy to ruin the landed interest in order to enrich monied and military men, and of being prepared to perpetuate hostilities to achieve their goals.

There was in fact no such conspiracy. The Whigs were as much dependent upon landed support as were the Tories. In a period when over half the House of Commons consisted of landowners they could not otherwise have gained significant representation there, much less achieve parliamentary majorities. Similarly, there were Tory financiers who speculated in government funds as eagerly as any Whig. Nevertheless, there was a redistribution of income between taxpayers, especially landowners, and state creditors during the wars against France, while Whigs were much more committed to those wars than were Tories. This was the basis of fact upon which Tory propagandists, including Jonathan Swift, constructed their conspiracy thesis.

Walpole, who was both a country gentleman and an astute financial administrator, was more aware than most of the social tensions which war finance had created. One of his main motives in pursuing a peaceful foreign policy was to keep the rate of the land tax well below its wartime level. Where this appealed to the landed interest, he also commanded the confidence of the City, as the area around the Bank became known in this period. He gained their respect through his handling of the South Sea Bubble in 1720, the greatest financial crisis since the Revolution. By a combination of luck and judgement he ensured the survival of the new system of public credit and of the institutions which serviced it. Walpole's financial ability was not the least important element in the establishment of political stability.[4]

The containment of the forces generated by the great issues of the succession, religion and continental war also assisted the forging of a working relationship between crown and parliament. Debates became less heated with the defusing of explosive questions, making both

Houses easier to manage. Parliamentary management also became less difficult to Walpole than it had been for previous ministers because of his more successful exploitation of the power of the crown to influence the votes of peers and MPs. Monarchs had at their disposal a wide range of administrative posts, for instance in their households and in the revenue system. These ranged from cabinet offices like that of first lord of the Treasury to sinecures such as the stewardship of the Chiltern Hundreds. Places in the gift of the crown had been used for ages to reward members of both Houses of Parliament for their loyalty. Under William and Anne between a fifth and a quarter of the Commons were so rewarded. During Walpole's ministry the proportion increased to about a third. Although they never amounted to an actual majority they undoubtedly enhanced the crown's influence in parliament.

Moreover, their behaviour became more predictable. Before 1714 the Whig and Tory parties alternated in office, and rewarded their supporters in parliament with places under the crown. Something like a spoils system began to operate in British politics. The result was that the placemen, as parliamentary beneficiaries of royal patronage were called, became a mixture of Tories and Whigs, with consequently mixed loyalties. For example, in 1705 several Tory placemen voted against the government in a key division when the ministry had instructed its supporters to vote for a Whig Speaker in the House of Commons.

After 1714 such rebellions became rarer. The seesawing of the two parties abruptly stopped, with the Whig end of the seesaw uppermost. Until Walpole's fall royal patronage was bestowed exclusively on Whigs. In the words of one historian, Britain became a single-party state.[5] One result of this was that the placemen in parliament became more reliable, so much so that they were called the Old Corps in recognition of their almost military discipline. Walpole thus mastered a machine which had frequently broken down under his predecessors.

Consequently, although the Revolution meant that monarchs had to work with parliament, this did not mean that the crown became a junior partner in the Constitution. On the contrary, in many ways George II was far more powerful ruling in conjunction with parliament than the later Stuarts had been when they tried to rule without it.

Another advantage which Walpole had over previous prime ministers was that he did not have to face the electorate anything like as frequently. The Triennial Act of 1694 required a general election to be held every three years, while between 1695 and 1715 they actually occurred on average every two years. This kept the country in an almost permanent state of electioneering, and did as much as anything to ensure continued political instability under William and Anne. In

1716 the Whigs passed the Septennial Act, extending the interval between elections to seven years. Moreover, parliaments were usually allowed to run their maximum length. Between 1720 and 1742 Walpole had to survive only four general elections, as many as had occurred between January 1701 and May 1705 alone.

The electoral system contributed to political stability in another way also. There was no notion of equal electoral districts, so that there was an enormous discrepancy between the largest constituencies, with thousands of voters, and the smallest, with a mere handful. Between the Revolution and the accession of the House of Hanover there was a struggle for control between Tories and Whigs in most constituencies. The influence of the crown could intervene decisively in the smaller boroughs by giving patronage to one side or the other. When it became clear after 1714 that only the Whigs were to receive its backing, many Tories gave up the unequal struggle. The result was that many boroughs fell into the hands of local Whig magnates who returned members loyal to Walpole. This ensured his ministry a majority at the polls even if the larger constituencies voted overwhelmingly for opposition MPs. As long as he retained the support of the Whig magnates in the localities Walpole could virtually ignore the electorate.

It is remarkable in retrospect that the electorate on the whole accepted the Septennial Act and acquiesced in the growth of oligarchy. One might have expected more protests against a political system which steadily became less representative under the early Hanoverians than it had been under the later Stuarts. To be sure, electors who had the chance of casting an independent vote, as many had in the counties and larger boroughs, tended to do so overwhelmingly for opposition candidates, while members representing such constituencies mounted campaigns for the repeal of the Septennial Act. Yet even when it became obvious that the system was loaded against them there are no signs of the construction of a radical platform to reform it, or of the disinherited resorting to unconstitutional methods of protest. True, one comes across occasional complaints against rotten boroughs, and even criticisms of the unrepresentative nature of the House of Commons. But these were not orchestrated into a genuinely radical programme until after 1760.[6] As for popular protest in the form of disturbances or riots, they actually seem to have diminished rather than grown under the first two Georges. Demonstrations of a high church Tory, if not of an overtly Jacobite hue, were commonplace in the years after Anne's death, and the government took them seriously enough to pass the Riot Act in an attempt to suppress them.[7] The Statute Book was also used by the Whig governments of George I's reign to suppress other activities which threatened the stability they sought. Most notoriously the so-called Waltham Black Act of 1723 added to an already bloody penal code which imposed the death penalty for theft and even for threatening behaviour.[8]

Still the fissures within the ruling class, and between it and the lower orders, which are discernible in the decade following the accession of the house of Hanover, did not develop into serious structural faults during Walpole's ministry. The first did not widen into a serious conflict of interests, despite opposition attempts to exploit it. Neither did the second deepen into class struggle. On the contrary, signs of cohesion binding together English society are more impressive than evidence of social strain. Of course demonstrations and riots were far from disappearing. Walpole was himself mobbed during the upheavals associated with the Excise Crisis in 1733, while the Gin Riots three years later were regarded as a serious threat to stability. They were, however, insignificant by contrast with the Porteous Riots of 1736 in Edinburgh, which did register that the Hanoverian regime had alienated its Scottish subjects to a dangerous degree.

The perhaps grudging acceptance of the Robinocracy in England has been attributed to social and economic trends which underpinned political stability.[9] Between 1650 and 1750 the tendency of the English population to multiply was held in check. During the late seventeenth century, indeed, the total numbers of people living in England and Wales seem actually to have fallen, and although a recovery set in during the early eighteenth century, the rate of growth did not become rapid until after 1750.[10] At the same time agricultural productivity improved so that, even though some produce was exported, the price of food declined during these decades. This led to a rise in real incomes which generated many economic activities. The extra spending power helped to fuel the Financial Revolution. It also facilitated the expansion of the professions which occurred at this time.[11] There might even have been a consumer boom to stimulate manufacturing.

The Robinocracy therefore ruled over a relatively affluent society. This contributed at least as much to the efforts of the prime minister himself to effect the transference from the Century of Revolution to the Age of Political Stability.

Further reading

Overviews: J.R. Jones, *Country and Court: England 1658–1714* (1976); W.A. Speck, *Stability and Strife: England 1714–1760* (1977). *Special studies*: Linda Colley, *In Defiance of Oligarchy: The Tory*

Party 1714–1760 (1982); J.P. Kenyon, *Revolution Principles: The Politics of Party 1689–1720* (1977); B. Lenman, *The Jacobite Risings in Britain 1689–1759* (1980); J.H. Plumb, *The Growth of Political Stability in England 1675–1725* (1967); J. Black, editor, *Britain in the Age of Walpole* (1985).

CHAPTER EIGHT

Love, Marriage and Death

Keith Wrightson

The faces of the rulers of early modern Britain are well known to us. The kings and queens, courtiers and councillors, admirals and generals – the history-makers on the grand scale – gaze down on us from the walls of the national portrait galleries or out of the pages of school textbooks. Aloof, distant, they are of another age, and yet they are part of our own consciousness too. Long dead, they remain human reference points in our charts of the past.

We know also the physiognomy of wealth, status and power. The nobles and gentlefolk who crowd the staircases and drawing rooms of stately homes, guardian spirits of the splendid edifices which they caused to be erected, possess less *individual* resonance. Yet they have a familiar *collective* countenance. We recognise their style and we sense what it meant, in the tilt of an aristocratic chin, or the level stare of a pair of patrician eyes. The 'theatre of the great' has lost little of the impressive power which was its purpose. It retains its capacity to dominate the historical imagination. We call it our National Heritage.

In contrast, the common people of the sixteenth and seventeenth centuries have small place in our conventional sense of the past. Farmers and craftsmen, labourers and servants, women and children, are altogether less historically *visible*. Britain has no direct equivalent of the scenes of Flemish peasant life painted by Breughel, or of the genre painting which portrays the streets and houses of the seventeenth-century Netherlands. Instead, we have only the crude woodcuts which illustrated the cheap literature of the period and occasional examples of clumsy vernacular sculpture. They can be vigorous, to be sure, but they are often coarse, flat, stereotyped images, revealing something of contemporary costume and manners, but little or nothing of individual character.

That this should be so is scarcely surprising. This was, after all, a

8.1. Detail of a Breughel painting showing peasant girls returning from the harvest

8.2. A crude woodcut showing peasants ploughing the fields

world in which the greater part of the population could be dismissed as people having 'neither voice nor authoritie in the common wealthe, but are to be ruled and not to rule other', or 'the inferior sort of people', who 'get their livelihood either in a mechanic, or servile way'.[1] Yet these people had their history too. Nor was it necessarily mute and inglorious. Indeed, in more than a few respects their historical experience is more relevant to our social and cultural heritage than that of those who cut a more conspicuous figure on the historical stage.

How can we approach that experience? We can do it above all by an imaginative employment of the surviving documentary evidence in which Britain is peculiarly rich. We may not know the faces of the common people, but we can reconstruct their lives, observe their actions and even hear their voices.

We have, for example, the parish registers which from the sixteenth century recorded the baptisms, marriages and burials of the inhabitants of thousands of villages and towns. After much painstaking analysis of the evidence which they provide we can state with some confidence that under Elizabeth and the early Stuarts, the average life expectation at birth of English villagers was in the region of thirty-eight years; that something like a fifth of all children born died in the first year of life; that a quarter to a third would fail to survive to the age of ten; that of those who reached adulthood, very few would see their sixtieth birthday. We know that on average they married not young, as was once thought, but in their mid-to-late twenties; that their marriages were broken by death as commonly as they are broken by divorce today, and that they remarried rapidly. We know that despite the prolonged celibacy between sexual maturity and their late marriages, they were inured to sexual restraint (for despite their lack of efficient contraception, illegitimacy levels were low). Such restraint, however, crumbled on the eve of marriage (for a high proportion of brides were certainly pregnant when they married). Moreover, we can establish not only the broadly enduring patterns of birth, marriage and death, but also the specific events which punctuated the demographic record. We can detect the statistical footprints of the plagues which periodically sent mortality soaring in the months of late summer, leaving individual families and whole communities devastated; or the rarer famines which could double or treble death rates in the winter after a bad harvest. The latter are revealed when dramatic increases in burials are accompanied by a simultaneous fall in the numbers of marriages and conceptions – couples were delaying their marriage plans till better times; sexual activity was declining; women suffering from malnutrition were losing their capacity to conceive.

The laconic entries of parish registers alone can thus be made to speak volumes. And we have also the manorial and estate records which allow us to reconstruct the anatomy of an essentially agrarian society, or the taxation records which provide a profile of the social and geographical distributions of wealth. At the level of the parish there are account books affording glimpses of the staging of a parish feast or a religious play, the maintenance of the poor, or the upkeep of the fabric and furniture of the church. At the level of the individual there are the wills and testaments of thousands of villagers and townspeople, usually dictated on their deathbeds and providing details of the transmission of their property and the care of their surviving spouses and children. Often enough, these are accompanied by intimately detailed inventories of goods. We can use these to explore both the household economies of farmers and craftsmen and to study changes in living standards. In the best of them we can pass literally from room to room in a long-vanished house, observing a cupboard here, a pewter candlestick there, a bedstead in the parlour, or a chicken scampering across the backhouse.

Again, we have the records of the courts: the local courts of manor, barony, county or borough, which dealt with everything from petty misdemeanours to serious crime; the church courts and kirk sessions which policed numerous moral and religious offences, as well as handling litigation over marriage, probate and defamation of character; the various central courts which heard civil or criminal cases and generated masses of recorded testimony, vividly illuminating the obscure dramas of provincial life. In their records we can hear the very voice of the age: the desperate Essex labourer who stole a sheep one winter night 'beinge a verie poore man and haveing a wiefe and seaven smale children and being very hungery'; the exasperated Durham father who confronted his daughter's dilatory suitor and urged him 'not to keep her in tigg tagg soo long'; the Wiltshire girl who regarded her vicar's sermons as 'such a deal of bibble babble that I am weary to hear yt and I can then sitt downe in my seat and take a good napp'.[2]

Each type of document can throw a penetrating torch beam into the dark corners of our historical knowledge. Even when terse and formal, they can prove extraordinarily illuminating in the reconstruction of individual lives. Few of the common people kept diaries or wrote autobiographies (though *some* did, and they are invaluable). Yet the annals of the poor are neither short nor simple. The scraps of evidence generated by individuals over a lifetime can be pieced together like a jig-saw puzzle to remarkable effect.

Take, for example, the life of Henry Abbot of Earls Colne in Essex, as reconstructed by Dr Alan Macfarlane.[3] Henry was born in 1564

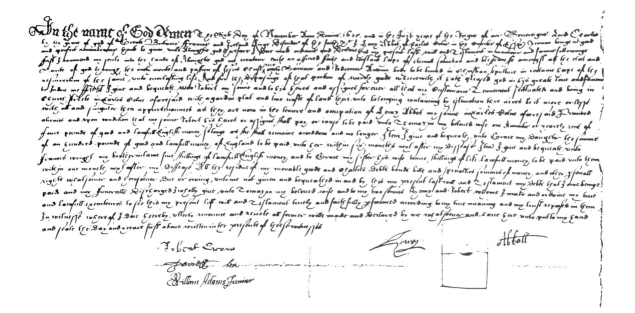

8.3 The will of Henry Abbot

and lived the remarkably long period of seventy-three years in Earls Colne. At four years old he lost his father. His mother remarried and he was apparently cared for by his uncles Henry and Robert, one of whom acted as trustee for the £6-13s-4d left to Henry by his father's will. Around 1589 he married Thomasine Culverton. He was twenty-five; she was only fifteen – an unusually young bride. In fact she was an orphan and her guardian was Henry's uncle Robert. Perhaps their marriage had been expected since childhood. She had inherited a little land and she and Henry probably lived by a mixture of farming and part-time employment in the local weaving trade. They had six children, three of whom predeceased them. In adult life Henry appeared frequently in the records of the manorial courts and in taxation listings. He acted as a witness for the wills of some of his neighbours and he was literate enough to sign his name. In middle life he had his share of trouble. On one occasion he was hauled before the church courts for allegedly making lewd remarks about one of his neighbours when he was drunk. He was involved in something of a feud with the lord of the manor and was at one point described by his opponents as 'a vile and troublesome member of the commonwealth'. He also took up the cudgels in defence of the old vicar of his parish, who was ousted by the squire in 1609. Perhaps as a result, he was a poor church attender. He was prosecuted in 1609 for 'great negligence in not frequenting his parish church in divine service time . . . and also that he doth seldom or never upon a sabbath day repair to evening prayer, but at such time he is walking up and down the fields'. Next year he was in trouble for *attending* church and interrupting the sermon of the new vicar, Mr Greenfield. He refused to sit in the place appointed for him by the churchwardens and took to walking out of church before the end of the sermon. He once compounded his offence by making a 'base and most filthy' gesture at the vicar as he did so. Clearly, Henry was no angel. However, we know that he became reconciled to Mr Greenfield and by the 1620s he was to all appearances a respectable village patriarch. He was elected ale-taster in 1625. And in his will he commended his soul 'into the hands of Almightie god my creatour With an assured Faith and constant hope of eternall salvation and blessednesse amongst all the elect and Saints of god'. He arranged for the maintenance of Thomasine, his 'beloved wife', set up his two surviving sons and left his daughter a large portion of £100. His obligations discharged, to the best of our knowledge he died at peace with God and man.

As these brief extracts from the life of Henry Abbot show, the surviving documentation of the lives of the common people of early modern Britain is vast in quantity and can be rich in quality. As yet it has been explored only partially – and much more for England than for Scotland or Wales. Nonetheless, enough is known to permit cautious generalisations about the texture of daily life in the period.

In the first place it was a predominantly rural society. The cycle of life was closely bound to the seasons of the agricultural year and the harvest was 'the heartbeat of the whole economy'.[4] Townspeople, of course, lived by trade, by the provision of services of various kinds and by the miscellaneous manufactures produced in small craft workshops. The role of the towns was vital. Yet they contained only a small, though growing, proportion of the population. Even the major manufacturing industries of the period were rurally based and their workers were often small farm or cottager families: the scythesmiths and nailers of the West Midlands; the yeoman clothworkers of South Lancashire; the straw-plaiters and lace-makers of Bedfordshire and Devon, or Henry and Thomasine Abbot and their children.

Secondly, it was a relatively small-scale world. By our standards Britain was thinly peopled. The bulk of the population lived their lives in what would seem to us tiny communities of a few hundred souls. Settlement patterns varied from the nucleated villages of the predominantly arable lowlands to the scattered hamlets and farms of the pastoral uplands, fens and forests. But the general scale was small. Even important towns were small by our reckoning and the capital cities of Edinburgh, and still more London, provided a quite exceptional metropolitan experience.

However, it would be quite wrong to assume that the rural communities of the period were static and cut off from the outside world. In fact people in early modern Britain rarely stayed in one settlement all their lives. Adolescents and young adults moved from master to master and parish to parish on annual contracts as farm servants. Families moved from place to place in search of land or work. In Cogenhoe, Northamptonshire, just over half of the inhabitants of 1628 had arrived in the parish since 1618. There was also a constant flow of migrants from country to town. London alone had death rates which meant that it needed some six to eight thousand new migrants each year to replace its losses and grow as it did from a city of around fifty thousand in 1500 to one of half a million people by 1700. In general, the effective 'social area' within which people lived extended for several miles beyond their parishes of residence, and in individual cases it could be quite extensive. Moreover, the myriad rural communities of provincial Britain were bound into a larger world by the institutions of church and state, by the economic links of the market, and also by the growing popular literacy which gave a large minority access to a broader world of news, information and ideas.

Be that as it may, life was centred on the locality. The basic unit of society was the household: an institution vital not only as the place of residence, consumption, reproduction and child-rearing, but also often enough as a unit of production and education. Most households were small in size and simple in structure – the nuclear family household consisting of a married couple and their children was already the norm. Yet an actual majority of the population lived in the larger households of the wealthiest third of the population, which included young servants and apprentices among their members. Beyond the household the lives of townspeople and villagers were focused by a constellation of local institutions – the manor, the parish, the craft fellowships or guilds – and by the ties of kinship and neighbourliness. Close relatives were undoubtedly significant sources of aid and support. They might take in orphaned children, for example, as in Henry Abbot's case. In general, however, villagers do not appear to have been intimately interrelated with one another by blood. The geographical mobility of the population precluded that by spreading family members over a quite extensive area. Beyond the immediate family, neighbourhood was the vital social tie and 'good neighbourliness' was a critically important social virtue. This is not to suggest that life was an idyll of neighbourly harmony. Neighbours quarrelled often enough, as Henry Abbot's chequered career makes plain. Yet neighbourliness meant something: a practical source of aid; a moral community of values. It was stressed in the religious duty of being 'in charity' with one's neighbours. It was expressed in the feasts and festivals which punctuated the year – Christmas mumming, maying,

8.4. Peasants dancing (detail from a Breughel painting)

the church ale, the parish wakes – in the informal recreations of the alehouse and the bowling green, and in the substantial gatherings of neighbours at weddings, christenings and funerals. What one contemporary called 'the mutuall comforts of neighbourhood' were the surest protection against the manifold insecurities of an uncertain world.[5]

This was, then, an intimate world. But it was also a profoundly unequal world. Inequalities of wealth, status and power vitally affected the experiences and life chances of individuals, and they were simply taken for granted, indeed justified as God-ordained. In society at large the fundamental distinction was that between 'gentlefolk' and the rest. Within local communities clear distinctions were recognised between the 'principal inhabitants' and the 'meaner sort', persons of 'good-credit' and persons of none. People sat in church in order of social rank, their places allocated by the parish officers. Deference to one's 'betters' was expected and could be enforced. Of course, not everyone displayed it. Henry Abbot showed a comprehensive disrespect for churchwardens, squire and parson alike. There were occasional risings and collective protests which helped to establish the terms on which subordination was accepted by the common people. There were also opportunities for individual social mobility within a limited range. Yet none of this altered the basic structures of social relations. Indeed, the relative social distance between rich and poor increased in the course of this period. Population expansion and economic change swelled the ranks of the labouring poor and whittled away those of the independent small farmers and craftsmen, while commercial opportunity enhanced the wealth and living standards of the fortunate and the enterprising.

Nor were distinctions of wealth and status the only ones to be recognised. This was a patriarchal society in theory and to a large extent in practice. Women were differentiated by social rank, but they shared the subordination of their sex. According to the Anglican homily on marriage, an official sermon read out periodically in parish churches, woman was 'the weaker vessel', 'a weak creature, not endued with the like strength and constancy of mind ... the sooner disquieted and ... the more prone to all weak affections and dispositions of the mind, more than men be'. Men and women, it was argued, 'should live in a perpetual friendship', but one based on female subordination.[6] Women were the helpmates and yokefellows of their menfolk, but not their equals. 'He is, as it were, the prince and chief ruler', wrote William Perkins of the household head, 'she is the associate'.[7] Moreover, authority was associated not only with rank and gender but also with age. Full adulthood came only with the economic independence which permitted marriage and the headship of a separate household. For some it was never achieved. In the later sixteenth century perhaps a tenth of the people who reached physical adulthood never married, since they were unable to obtain such independence. In the hard times of the seventeenth century the proportion may have been as high as a quarter.

These are some of the cold facts of life in early modern Britain. But if life could be hard, it was not without satisfactions. Nowhere is this

8.5. Bread distribution to the poor

more apparent than in the sphere of family life. Accounts of the family which stress its separateness from our own experience – the arranged marriage, the lack of emotional involvement of spouses with one another, the authoritarian subordination of children – have been heavily qualified by accumulating knowledge of the realities of family life. Parents certainly expected to be involved in the matchmaking of their children, at least to the extent of giving their consent. Partners to a match were expected to display a rough 'parity' with regard to wealth, social standing, age and personal reputation. But all this still left plenty of room for individual choice. Young people found their own sweethearts, even if it was important to secure parental 'goodwill'. Emotional factors were at least as important as material prudence in choosing a spouse and could indeed take precedence. The attitudes involved are admirably encapsulated in the account of his elder brother's courtship written by Adam Martindale, a Lancashire yeoman's son. Their father expected his son to marry prudently and was well pleased when he courted a young woman 'of suitable years' and good character, who also had a marriage portion of £140. To the grief of his family, however, the son threw her over when he fell for 'a young, wild airy, girle . . .; a huge lover and frequenter of wakes, greenes and merrie-nights where musick and dancing abounded. And as for her portion it was onely forty pounds.' The family strove to dissuade him, but 'say and do what we could, he was uncounsellable, have her he would'. And have her he did, after winning his father's reluctant consent – and as it happened, 'she proved, above all just expectation, not onely civill, but religious and an exceeding good wife' as Martindale grudgingly admitted.[8]

The villagers of the early modern period had every reason to be prudent when they married – there was no true divorce for them – but they were no strangers to romantic passion. The apprentice Roger Lowe, who left a remarkable account of his courtships between 1663 and 1668, was a case in point. His breast swelled with romantic impulses. With one sweetheart he 'ingaged to be faithful till death' and was justifiably aggrieved when she dropped him without explanation. He did better with his future wife, Emm Potter, whom he first approached in an alehouse during the town wakes week after conceiving 'a most ardent affection'. They courted on and off for four years before they amassed the wherewithal to accomplish what he called their 'grand designe of mariage'.[9] It was a situation familiar enough to be parodied in the chapbook dialogue *Andrew and his sweetheart Joan*, which portrayed two servants sitting up late at night and running over their marital prospects. They had accumulated some savings and basic household utensils and they loved each other dearly. 'I love thee more than a Bear does Honey', declares Andrew, 'And I hope you'l affect me as much as a Sow does a bunch of Carrots.'[10]

If courtship among the common people was relatively free and undoubtedly romantic, relations within marriage and between parents and children were far less characterised by distance, deference and low expectation of emotional fulfilment than was once thought. The husband could be formally defined as 'he that hath authority over the wife', but in practice men were often far less dominant and women far more assertive than official values allowed.[11] Moreover, formal male authority was not incompatible with love, though it clearly ruled out true equality. In the final analysis marriages involved a fundamental co-operation of man and wife in the struggle to sustain their families and this could breed close emotional bonding and a dogged companionship. There is deep respect in the declaration of one dying man, 'that what estate he had, he together with his wife Jane had got it by their industry and therefore he gave and bequeathed all . . . to be at her disposall, and that if it were more (she) deserved it well'.[12] Nor was he alone. Again, parents were demonstrably aware of their duties to love, protect, raise and guide their children. There is none of the emotional coolness and even negligence alleged by some historians; in the recorded statement of one North Country labourer when he took his newborn child in his arms: 'Honny thou's my Darlin' and shalt want for nothing as long as I am able to warke for thee'.[13] There is none of the supposed indifference to infant life in the grief of the diarist who wrote on his child's death, 'the grief for this child was so great that I forgot myself so much that I did offend God . . . for I was much distracted in my mind and could not be comforted'.[14] Parents, then as now, found children a source of expense, anxiety and sometimes distress. But they also found in them great emotional satisfaction. Witness this description of a two-year-old at play: 'We had a wanton tearing calfe, that would runne at children to beare them over. This calfe he would encounter with a sticke in his hand . . . stand his ground stoutly, beat it back and triumph over it . . . I doe not think one child of 100 of his age durst doe so much.' The child in question had died years before his father committed this proud memory to paper.[15]

Premature death came all too often in early modern Britain. Yet in the face of death the bonds of family and neighbourhood came to the fore. People died at home, and in public, often surrounded by family and friends. They settled their material and emotional obligations as best they could – a matter which could involve complex negotiations with heirs and successors. That achieved, they endeavoured to die well, with dignity and resolution, supported by the presence of those they held dear and the promises of their religion. They often specified where they wished to be buried – near a deceased spouse or kinsfolk –

and they were accompanied to the grave by large bodies of their neighbours, who ate and drank together in the churchyard after the interment. To be 'brought forth honestly among the neighbours' mattered. It was a final demonstration of a community which embraced the living and the dead.

Life in early modern Britain was often materially poor. Yet it could be emotionally rich. The attitudes and beliefs of the time are in many ways alien to us. Yet they can be familiar too. When we can hear the voices of the people of the time they often convey a common humanity which crosses the centuries as effectively as the poetry of Shakespeare or Milton. Those voices deserve to be heard, if only to place in perspective the sound and fury of the celebrations of power which we call our history.

Further reading

K. Wrightson, *English Society 1580–1680* (London, 1982); P. Laslett, *The World We Have Lost – further explored* (London, 1984); R. Houlbrooke, *The English Family 1450–1700* (London, 1984); M. Spufford, *Contrasting Communities. English Villagers in the sixteenth and seventeenth centuries* (Cambridge, 1974); R. Gough, *The History of Myddle*, ed. D. Hey (Penguin Books, Harmondsworth, 1981); R. Mitchison, *Life in Scotland* (London, 1978).

CHAPTER NINE

Buying and Selling

Margaret Spufford

At the beginning of the sixteenth century the vast majority of the English people lived in the countryside. Most of them, below the level of the gentry, with the exception of the yeoman farmers, were constantly engaged in the struggle to stay alive. The struggle for basic shelter and food took up most of their lives. Most material possessions which we think of as necessities would have been unimaginable to them. Two hundred years later, at the beginning of the eighteenth century, not only could they afford these necessities, but they could also buy goods once seen as inconceivable luxuries – bedlinen, pewter bowls and plates, even books and newspapers. This prosperity was the product of agricultural and population change and resulted in a dramatic rise in living standards.

The magnitude of these changes is difficult for us to grasp just because they involve possessions that are so basic that we take them for granted. We do, of course, have the problem of the homeless and the vagrants, especially in big cities. On the whole, we tend to assume that we all live in permanent buildings, and that these houses have hot and cold water. We assume that we will have beds, with mattresses, and that on these beds will be sheets, which we can change when they get dirty. We assume that we will have at least two shirts to our backs, and that these, too, can be changed. We assume that we will eat meat, at least once a week, have butter on our bread, tea to put in the teapot and sugar to put in the tea when it is poured out. We assume there will be tobacco to smoke. We grumble when the chancellor of the exchequer slaps extra tax on wines and spirits, as well as beer, although we do not assume these things quite as we take tea and sugar for granted.

In the sixteenth century none of these assumptions would have been made. But a change in the way people lived had started. That change is my subject. It can be traced only because of the survival of hundreds of thousands of probate inventories, made not only after the deaths of ordinary people, except the very poor, but also after the deaths of shopkeepers, and even pedlars. The best of these record a man's goods in intimate detail, so we may observe his furnishings, or see what he stocked in the shop, or rolled in the pedlar's pack, before going out of doors to inspect the crops growing on the land, and count the animals huddled in the yard. So we can trace changes in furnishings, or farming practices, or even shop goods, over time.

William Harrison wrote in 1577 about the change that had already happened in his part of Essex, during the lives of old people who had talked to him:

> There are old men yet dwelling in the village where I remain which have noted three things to be marvellously altered in England within their sound remembrance ... one is the multitude of chimneys lately erected, whereas in their young days there were not above two or three, ... in most uplandish towns of the realm. ...
>
> The second is the great ... amendment of lodging, for (said they) our fathers, yea, and we ourselves also, have lain full often on straw pallets on rough mats covered only with a sheet ... and a good round log under their heads instead of a bolster or pillow ... pillows (said they) were thought meant only for women in childbed. As for servants, if they had any sheet above them it was well, seldom had they any under their bodies to keep them from the pricking straws that ran often through the canvas of the pallet. ...
>
> The third thing they tell of is the exchange of vessel, as of treen [wooden] platters into pewter and wooden spoons into silver or tin. For so common were all sort of trine stuff in old time that a man should hardly find four pieces of pewter ... in a good farmer's house.[1]

So to Harrison, the appearance of chimneys, comfortable bedding, including pillows and sheets, and pewter plates, dishes and spoons, was all remarkable, and remarked amongst the humble.

Richard Carew, who wrote his *Survey of Cornwall* in the 1580s, described the houses of husbandmen, that is farmers of medium-sized or traditional farms like this. They had

> walles of earth, low thatched roofes, few partitions, no planchings or glasse windowes, and scarecely any chimnies, other than a hole in the wall to let out the smoke: their bed, straw and a blanket: as for sheets, so much linen cloth had not yet stepped over the narrow channell between them and Britanny (Brittaine).[2]

To start at the beginning, with the house. We know from archaeologists that in the medieval period, at least in the Yorkshire village of Wharram Percy, even housing was not permanent for the villagers. The Wharram Percy houses were rebuilt every generation or so.[3] Richard Carew, in the 1580s, was describing the sort of house that would not survive. But the sixteenth century saw a change so great, at least amongst the houses of the yeomanry, the largest farmers, that it is known amongst historians as the 'Great Rebuilding'. The account book of Robert Loder, yeoman, of Berkshire details his expenses in 1618 when he added to his house. He put in a chimney, staircase and window glass, just as Harrison had suggested Essex yeomen were doing, and in all 'Money layd out aboute my Chimney ... [and] making my staires my window and selling and plastering' cost him nearly £40,[4] a huge sum when a day labourer was paid under a shilling a day. At the beginning of this change, window glass was so special that it was listed separately in the inventory made after a man's death.

The inventory of the goods of Nicholas Hill, a baker of Whitney in Oxfordshire was taken after his death in 1590. Not only does it list the glass in the parlour window, but Nicholas had a feather bed and bolster and 'old sheete' in his parlour, along with a tablecloth and napkins, pewter plates and pots in his buttery.[5] The view from the new parlour window may have been greenish coloured: as is surviving seventeenth-century glass from round the furnace where it was blown in Eccleshall in Staffordshire.

In the fen village of Willingham, in Cambridgeshire, in 1603 Thomas Greaves lived in one of these improved houses. He belonged to a family which included relatively prosperous yeomen at one end of the scale and labourers at the other.[6] Increasing prosperity came to the larger farmers because, as we now know from analysing the parish registers, the population of England nearly doubled between 1550 and 1650.[7] There was a very steep rise between the 1550s and the 1650s, and then the population level stabilised. All these extra people to feed meant that the price of food, especially basic bread grains, shot up. In the half century to 1600 the price of grain more than tripled. Barley, which was bread flour for ordinary people, rose ninefold in price by the 1630s. This price rise gave the yeoman who had a surplus to sell his great opportunity, especially in years of bad harvest. Robert Loder stored his surplus from the bumper crop of 1619, and sold it three years later when the harvest was bad, at twice the value. This was the reason for his prosperity, and that of men like Thomas Greaves, living in substantial newly built or extended village houses, although at the time Robert Loder put his good fortunes down to the favours of Almighty God, not to his superior marketing techniques.[8]

9.1. The village of
Willingham, showing
the houses and their
closes

But of course while prosperous farmers with surplus to sell
benefited, people at the bottom end of rural society, the labourers on a
fixed wage, suffered. Some were so poor that they took to the roads
and wandered long distances in search of work. No wonder the
Elizabethans were so afraid of vagrants that they magnified the
problem out of all proportion, and also evolved the new Poor Law of
1601. However, the very presence of all these extra mouths to feed
was a tremendous stimulus to agricultural improvement. Instead of
bringing in shiploads of corn from the Baltic, why not grow more?
Thus what historians argue about as the 'agricultural revolution of the
seventeenth century' came about.[9]

In 1613, Robert Loder, who later extended his house at such
expense, was experimenting with vetches, leguminous crops which
would improve the fallow, on his open field farm. He was specialising,

as well. In 1617 his orchards produced over 2000 lbs of cherries, besides those his family ate and what he gave away. His maid spent 28 days at market selling them, and they brought him in £12 clear. Such specialised crops were grown in the market gardens and orchards especially to feed the new huge London which had grown up. By 1710, we have illustrations of pedlars who sold only cherries, or asparagus, to this luxury market.

Probably the single most important innovation in this 'agricultural revolution' was the introduction of new grasses,[10] above all sainfoin and clover. Gentlemen like Richard Weston were writing enthusiastically about them in the 1640s. When Robert Plot wrote his *Natural History of Oxfordshire* in 1677, he said in his typically irritating manner, that the new grasses were now 'everywhere grown, and so nothing of it', leaving us to infer their effects. But these were very considerable. Between 1580 and 1640, a middle-sized flock of sheep on a farmer's death in Oxfordshire contained only 14 animals. Between 1660 and 1730, it was four times the size.[11] All these extra animals would have fed on the new grasses. In turn, they produced more dung to fertilise the ground, helping to solve what was the main problem before artificial fertilisers came in. More fertile ground meant bigger crops of grain. So we may deduce a transformation of agriculture here.

Furthermore, when the population steadied at last in the 1650s, food prices steadied too. Grain prices actually dropped by about a fifth, even though the population was nearly twice the size, and meat, butter and egg prices all stayed stable between the 1650s and the 1740s. So we know the new, larger population was being adequately fed. England even became a considerable exporter of grain at the beginning of the eighteenth century. The only food prices that went on rising were those of animals on the hoof. If the price of a pig went up, but the price of pork per pound did not, I think we are entitled to deduce that the pig had got bigger. Therefore as well as turning into a grain exporter because she was growing more, England was also producing bigger, better animals, and improving breeding. Stable population, bigger grain yields and the bigger pig between them put an end to some of the misery sixteenth-century inflation had brought to all but the biggest farmers.

The prosperity which had been confined to yeomen spread downwards through rural society, even if it did not reach the very bottom. The labourer's wages brought more in his shopping basket, and suddenly the relatively poor were also in a position to buy new small luxuries. Not all of them were so small. It was now the turn of the labourers to improve their houses.

Seventeenth-century three-roomed cottages survive in large numbers

9.2. Yeoman farmers' homes in Chippenham

in eleven counties of eastern England. In the Banbury region of Oxfordshire the three-roomed cottage was 'the important, if not the basic' form. When the landlords at Chippenham, in Cambridgeshire, created themselves a park in the 1690s, which was mapped in 1712, they built a terrace of model cottages in 'New Street' to provide housing for the humbler tenants, the landless labourers who had been dispossessed of their houses in the old village. A couple of these houses were still standing, down at the bottom of the park, when the map was made. These new cottages, with their upper storeys, glassed windows and massive brick chimney stacks, were a far cry from the impermanent houses their forebears in a similar situation would have lived in. They incorporated all the improvements Harrison had noted among the yeomen in Essex a little over a hundred years before. Presumably they reflected the expectations a seventeenth-century labourer might reasonably have. Moreover, their interiors were differently furnished. Not only did the wage labourer have glass in his windows, but he quite often had window curtains as well.

The probate inventories from four different counties in England, spreading from East Anglia to the borders of Wales,[12] show that one of the most dramatic changes among the poorer sections of society represented was their possession of what might be called 'soft furnishings'. Above all, they could change the sheets; those sheets which, you remember, Richard Carew had pointed out did not exist at all in Cornwall in the 1580s. Yeomen had had linen in quantity since the sixteenth century; Henry Best of Yorkshire wrote out a washing list in 1640.[13] William Crisp, who came from Willingham, from a family very like the Greaves, whose house was mentioned earlier, had nine pairs of sheets and a dozen pillowcases in his 'little' parlour in 1670.

He also had newfangled innovations. His joint bedstead with its feather bed in the parlour had a pair of curtains and a valence as well. There were seven leather chairs in the same room. It is even more impressive that the poverty-stricken husbandman Francis Adams, of Willingham, whose goods were worth only £5, and whose debts, for which he had signed bonds, amounted to more than that sum, had amongst his meagre possessions five pillows, six pillowcases (of which one was made of imported linen from Holland and four were flaxen) and two pairs of flaxen sheets. He also had no less than nine pairs of coarse hempen sheets, as well as four napkins. William Harrison, who wrote in the 1570s that only women in childbirth had pillows, would have been astonished.

How had this change in domestic comfort come about? Although historians argue about the state of the roads in seventeenth-century England, and the volume of goods which were carried on them, there is no doubt that between 1637 and 1715 there was a remarkable growth in the number of regular carriers' services out from the capital to the provinces.[14] That is to say, you could go to the 'Bell Inn' in Wood Street on a regular day of the week, and expect to find a carrier's service leaving for Shrewsbury. The 'Saracen's Head' in Friday Street served Hereford. William Stout, shopkeeper, of Lancaster, came down to the 'Swan with Two Necks' in Lad Lane in 1695. A gentlewoman living in Bedfordshire could grumble to her fiancé in the 1650s that his letters were not coming through on the carrier's cart when it arrived every Thursday. A much more humble person, a Quaker, John Whiting, who was incarcerated in Ilchester Jail in Somerset for his beliefs in the 1680s, wrote quite casually of a 'parcel of Quaker books' which were regularly left for him at the inn by the carrier. The distribution network inside England had responded to a greater demand for the new products and developed a regular delivery service.

This delivery service had new outlets, too. The author of *The Trade of England Revived* in 1681 was complaining about them. He wanted to keep shopkeepers, specialist drapers, mercers, grocers, and so on, trading only in cities and market towns as they had traditionally done. Now, he wrote, 'in every country village where is (it may be) not above ten houses there is a shopkeeper'.[15] Although he undoubtedly exaggerated for effect, the general shop did indeed get much more common after 1660. We may tell how diversified its goods were by the detailed list of the goods of James Leach, of Bury in Lancashire, who ran an Aladdin's cave of a general shop in 1668. He had a wide variety of textiles and all the thimbles, pins, hooks and eyes, needles and threads a customer would need for making them up, and cheap lace, tape and ribbon for decorating the finished products as well as

soap and starch for washing them. He had knitted stockings at
different prices for men, women and children. He also had groceries.
Tea from India was there, and so was sugar from the Americas, both
white and brown. Cheap tobacco from the Americas was there too,
and so were the pipes to smoke it in. If you wanted to drink spirits
instead of beer, you could buy them from James Leach. If you felt
more intellectual, you could buy white paper from him for writing on
and books to read, and ready-made candles for reading by. If you
suffered from eye strain as a result, you could even purchase a pair of
spectacles at 2d apiece to help. Most of the goods necessary to clothe
and feed the body and even to entertain the mind could in fact be
found in James Leach's provincial general shop in 1668. He was not
at all unusual. What was unusual was the appearance, in a few shops
in Kent at the end of the seventeenth century, of ready-made complete
suits of clothes.[16] There indeed, was a foretaste of things to come, but
even James Leach in Bury stocked items that would have been an
outrageous luxury to most of the population a century earlier.

Another main complaint made by the author of *The Trade of
England Revived* was about the increasing number of pedlars on foot,
or chapmen, who swarmed about the country, taking goods directly to
people's doors. The pedlar was a well-established figure even in the
middle ages and very well known when Shakespeare, in 1611,

9.3. A shop interior

described the silver-tongued salesman Autolycus, who sold courtship presents, ballads, gloves, headgear, ribbons, laces and above all fabrics, to the shepherds of the sheep-shearing feast, in *The Winter's Tale*. Examination of the inventories listing the contents of the enormously heavy packs the pedlars carried round the country during the seventeenth century shows that they contained, above everything else, quantities of assorted cheap linens in different qualities and at varying prices. These men were the distributors of the fabrics to make the new sheets, shirts and window curtains that we can often trace in increased number in the inventories of the poorer people in society. And they were on the increase during the seventeenth century: over 2500 of them took out licences when they were taxed in 1697.

They catered for the gentry, as well as for the poor. Autolycus carried masks, perfume and poking sticks for ruffs in his pack. The household account book of the Bacon family in Stiffkey, in Norfolk, contains purchases of needles, ribbons and garters, cheap lace and cloth aprons in the 1590s. In the 1690s Sir Daniel Fleming of Rydal Hall, near Ambleside, showed his wife and daughter regularly purchasing from pedlars. They were indefatigable people at smelling out a market: Roland Johnson, who died in 1683, worked out from Penrith. Cumberland could scarcely be defined as one of the most prosperous areas of Britain. Yet from Johnson the local purchaser could buy Hollands and cambric coming from the Low Countries; Bengals, calicos and muslins from India; silks and linens dyed in England; light cloth from Scotland as a cheap alternative to calico for the newfangled window curtains; and gloves, muffs, lace, ribbons and combs for warmth and adornment. Since the purchaser could also stock up on the less transportable tea, sugar, tobacco and spirits in shops like that of James Leach in Bury, we know that the new goods from the Americas and India – tobacco, sugar and cottons – did indeed reach humble levels of society.

Because the pedlars worked out from London, and because they sold to all levels of society, they were also prime spreaders of news, rumour, gossip and cheap print. And there was a good deal of news in seventeenth-century England, including war news. There was also a newly literate public to read it. The printers catering for the just-literate had a new mass market. The spread of literacy was patchy, but in eastern England at least it had had a great boost in the 1580s. We can only measure literacy by the ability to write one's name, and in 1642 only 30 per cent of adult men could do that. But reading in the seventeenth century, unlike today, was taught before writing as a quite separate skill. It was not on the curriculum for girls at all. Alderman Newton of Cambridge was so proud of his son when he moved to the Grammar School at seven and learnt the new skill of writing in six months that he let him record the event in his own diary. The entry makes a very striking contrast with his father's scrawl.[17]

Children could start to earn by seven years old at the latest, and so, not unnaturally, all but the sons of yeomen left school at that age, and never learnt to write their names at all. Lists of signatures give us only an absolute minimum of those who could write, and tell us nothing about the spread of reading ability. However, we happen to know this whole fen community was interested in schooling, because we still have the list of those who subscribed money to pay a schoolmaster in perpetuity in 1593; it includes cottagers, contributing as much as a full year's rent in some cases, as well as yeomen like the Greaves family. Just as Thomas Greaves can be used as an example of a yeoman who benefited from the price rises of the sixteenth century and lived in a house which suited a very prosperous villager, so also can he be used as an example of the yeomen whose fathers could afford to keep their sons on at school after they were seven to acquire the skill of writing. In the 1620s and 1630s, Thomas Greaves wrote a group of wills for his fellow villagers. He was only one of a group of yeomen who had learnt to write at the village school, and so acted as village scribe. Some of the sons of cottagers who had subscribed to the school, and therefore were entitled to free teaching, learnt to read there before they were physically strong enough to start paid work.[18] So they too must have formed part of the new market for cheap print. By the 1660s material for these barely literate people, who could only read but not write, was pouring off the printing presses.

During the Civil War the newspapers had become increasingly important. A painter-stainer of Norwich made a sketchbook which survived. It includes a drawing of a pedlar selling his papers, and his audience spelling one out and arguing over it. It has been suggested that English society, with that of the Low Countries, was the most politically aware in Europe in the seventeenth century.

It was also the most commercially aware. Even the small purchases undertaken at the bottom end of society were made on credit. The pedlars and general shopkeepers who sold the new goods themselves bought stock on credit. 'Bills and bonds in the book' are a very frequent item in the probate inventories of the yeomen and widows who acted as moneylenders in rural society. None of them survived, but we do have instructions about how to draw up a bond in a cheap book which sold at 2d. There was so much indebtedness in English rural society that it must have acted as a very powerful incentive to scholarship to be able to read the bond which mortgaged the labourer's cottage, or the husbandman's land or goods, away, as happened to Francis Adams in 1672.

But there was more frivolous reading matter too. The ballads Autolycus sold at the beginning of the century were being replaced by the cheap books which Bunyan, the tinker's son, so much regretted reading in his youth in the 1640s.

> Give me a News-book ... *George* on Horseback, or *Bevis of Southamptron* ... give me some book that teaches curious Arts, that tells old Fables.

These books were reading for pure entertainment. Almanacs were the most useful publications. They not only prognosticated the future, but also served as pocket diaries. Henry Best of Yorkshire marked off his farming chores, as he performed them, on his almanac. By the 1660s they were so popular that one was printed for every three families in the kingdom. An almanac for women appeared from 1658. By 1685 there was even an almanac for the very pedlars or chapmen who distributed cheap goods. The title page of one copy which survives from 1688 lists amongst other useful information all the market days for each county in England and Wales.[19] And along with the improved distribution system and increasing number of carriers' carts rolling out of London to the provinces went improved maps.

One of the most popular of the new small luxuries were the printed hankerchiefs sold by the pedlar, not for blowing the nose of the customer, but for him or her to display. These silk handkerchiefs also carried choice political information or propaganda in the early eighteenth century. One supplies details of the clauses of the Treaty of Utrecht. Another has pictures illustrating Dr Sacheverell's trial. Significantly, the earliest of all of them to survive is a silk handkerchief from 1688. It showed not only a map of England with the road system on it but also, on the borders, market towns with the market day of each. England's communications were better; the country was getting smaller; and the poorer rural customers could and did not only buy new goods to furnish their houses, but even sport negligently in their top pockets, or around their necks, silk handkerchiefs displaying this new England.

Further reading

Agriculture: Joan Thirsk (ed.), *The Agrarian History of England and Wales*, IV, *1500–1640* (Cambridge, 1967) and V, *1640–1750* (Cambridge, 1985).
Housing: W.G. Hoskins, *Provincial England* (London, 1965).
Literacy and cheap print: Bernard Capp, *Astrology and the Popular*

9.4. Silk handkerchief commemorating the Treaty of Utrecht, 1713

9.5. Arguing over the newspaper outside a cobbler's shop in Norwich

9.6. Printed silk handkerchief *c.* 1680 showing roads and listing market towns and days

Press: English Almanacs, 1500–1800 (London, 1979); David Cressy, *Literacy and the Social Order: Reading and Writing in Tudor and Stuart England* (Cambridge, 1980).

Source materials: Collections of probate inventories are in print for many counties. See for instance, *Yeomen and Colliers in Telford: Probate Inventories for Dawley, Lilleshall, Wellington and Wrockwardine, 1660–1750*, ed. Barnie Trinder and Jeff Cox (Chichester, 1980).

Trade, shops and consumption: Margaret Spufford, *The Great Reclothing of Rural England: Petty Chapmen and their Wares in the Seventeenth Century* (Hambledon, 1984); Joan Thirsk, *Economic Policy and Projects: The Development of a Consumer Society in Early Modern England* (Oxford, 1978) especially ch. 5, 'The Quality of Goods and the Quality of Clients'; T.S. Willan, *The Inland Trade* (Manchester, 1976), especially ch. 3, 'Provincial Shops in the Seventeenth Century'.

Language and Literature:
Caxton to the Royal Society

Elizabeth Cook

During the sixteenth and seventeenth centuries England was engaged in intellectual, as well as territorial, expansion. The discovery of the new world opened up fresh trade routes for the export of home products such as woollen cloth and the import of such commodities as tobacco and potatoes (then thought aphrodisiac). But the expansive exchange of the period went beyond such measurable items. Words were acquired and exchanged along with commodities and information. Shakespeare's late play *The Tempest*, written around 1611, presents some of the issues and problems of colonialism. Prospero, providentially, as he sees it, shipwrecked on the island 'To be the lord on 't' (V.i.162), makes the native islander Caliban his slave. Prospero wins from Caliban the knowledge of 'the qualities o' th' isle' which he needs in order to survive (I.ii.339). In exchange he teaches Caliban his language – the coloniser's most enduring mark but a gift which a slave may question: 'You taught me language; and my profit on't / Is, I know how to curse. The red plague rid you / For learning me your language!' (I.ii.365).

The language which the colonisers (missionaries, merchants, settlers, exported, was itself expanding at an unprecedented rate. The period between the end of the fifteenth century (when the first printing presses were set up in this country) and the Restoration in 1660 witnessed the growth of English into a language capable of expressing all that its users might wish. 'I like our language', writes George Herbert, Anglican priest and poet, in the 1620s, 'Who cannot dresse it well, want wit, not words' ('The Sonne').

Latin had been, and to some extent continued to be, the international language of learning. The teaching of Latin through the 'best' classical texts formed a large part of the curricula of the new public and grammar schools such as St Pauls, founded by John Colet in 1509. The poet and parliamentarian Andrew Marvell served Cromwell as Latin Secretary – a post which he took over from John Milton in 1657. The so-called 'benefit of clergy' – which had come to mean 'benefit of those literate in Latin' – which allowed exemption from trial for certain offences on the reading of a 'neck-verse' in Latin was still available. It was still worth learning Latin if it could save your neck. But in the early seventeenth century one hears the learning of Latin being justified for the understanding it gives of the *English* language;[1] its worth is no longer self-evident. Thomas Hobbes and Francis Bacon, writing in the middle of the seventeenth century, publish much of their work in two forms: English for home readership, Latin for the continent. A century earlier the writing of serious philosophy in English would have been inconceivable. In 1643 John Milton published *The Doctrine and Discipline of Divorce* in English out of 'the esteem I have of my countries judgement, and the love I beare to my native language'.[2] Later he regretted it. Had he published in Latin the reaction would have been less. Latin had become the language which limited, rather than expanded, your readership.

The new literate – who, with the advent of printing, had more to read – also contained the newly wealthy: the merchant class. Many of the wealthier merchants directly involved themselves in the educational process by giving endowments to grammar schools. Adult education was also taking off. From 1597 free public lectures were given at Gresham College in London, formed by the Mercers with an endowment from the merchant/financier Thomas Gresham. These lectures – in Music, Physic, Geometry, Astronomy, Rhetoric, Divinity and Law – were to be given in Latin for the benefit of foreigners, but also in English 'forasmuch as the greatest Part of the Auditorie is like to bee of such Citizens and others as have small Knowledge, or none at all, of the Latine tongue'.[3]

There were those, physicians in particular, who resented the encroachment into their privileged territory which was threatened by the writing – or translation – of medical texts into the vernacular. Physicians and horticulturalists can still use Latin and Greek names to impress and keep ignorant those suffering from such ordinary and native maladies as chicken-pox or potato blight (*varicella* and *phytophthora infestans*). The move into the vernacular was part of a democratisation of knowledge that some, inevitably, resented. The translation of the Bible, together with the Reformation which had shifted the centre of authority from Christ's Church to God's Word, was the most consequential of all these democratising moves. It made the English Revolution possible.

And there was more knowledge to democratise: knowledge of an empirical, practical nature about the contemporary world, archeological knowledge about the past and, as a result of humanist scholarship, a greater knowledge of past literatures. One of the original meanings of the word 'translate' is 'to move from one place to another'. (One still speaks of the 'translation' of a saint's relics from one monastery to another in the middle ages; a process usually accomplished by theft which seemed to leave the magical qualities of the holy parts unimpaired.) The sixteenth and seventeenth centuries can be described as a time of great translation. It was a period of great literary translation: Virgil, Homer, Ovid, Plutarch, Thucydides (to name some great classical texts), Castiglione, Montaigne, Rabelais (to name some more modern), were all 'Englished' during these two centuries.[4] So was the Bible.[5] And while texts were being carried over into the vernacular the newly invented telescopes and microscopes carried the eye over great distances or into intricate cellular structures to reveal complexities of worlds previously unregarded because invisible. The mariner's compass carried voyagers into new lands and these voyagers carried home, not only new commodities and curios (in a sinister way Shakespeare's Caliban is considered marketable by the sailors who find him), but also information about different kinds of people, other ways of living. All this new information was translated and recorded in language. At a time before photographic reproduction the accuracy of verbal records in such areas of discovery was particularly important.

The vernacular received all this new information and expanded accordingly. The address to the reader of John Gerarde's *Herball* (first published in 1597) acknowledges Gerarde's gift to the *language* as well as to the eye and mind:

> Many things hath he nourished in his garden, and obserued in our English fieldes that neuer came into [others'] pens to write of. Againe, the greatest number of these plants, hauing neuer beene written of in the English toong, would haue wanted names for the vulgar sort to call them by: in which defect, he hath been curiously carefull, touching both old and new names to make supplie.[6]

The variousness of Gerarde's naming does as much as his meticulous and lovely illustrations to make us see distinctions between species: the 'Purple circled Daffodill', the 'Timely purple ringed Daffodill',

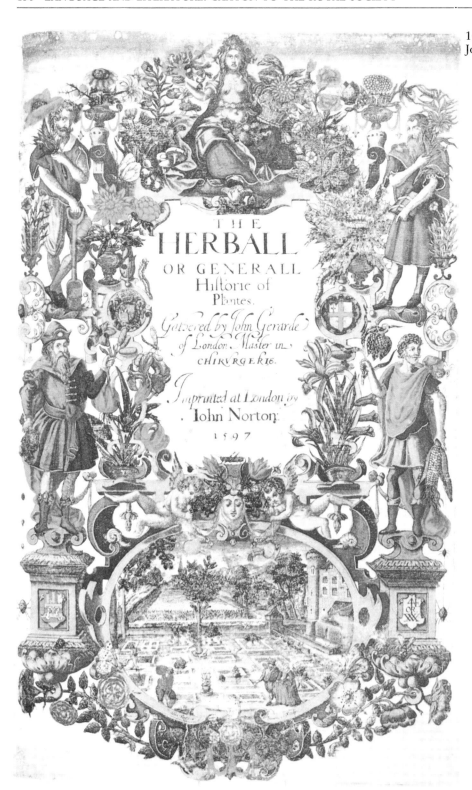

10.1. Frontispiece to
John Gerarde's *Herball*

'The verie hastie flowring Daffodill', 'Primrose peerles', the 'Milke white Daffodill'.[7]

This was a time of experiment, of testing. First-hand particular experience came increasingly to be valued as the only authentic basis for knowledge. Authorities who had gone unchallenged for centuries were now refuted in this new atmosphere of experimental enthusiasm. Anatomy is a case in point. Because of the divorce between medical theory and practical surgery – which had been regarded as more or less a labourer's job, delegated to barbers – the authority of the second-century Greek physician Galen had hardly been questioned before the sixteenth century. It took the Flemish physician Andreas Vesalius to test Galen's descriptions against the structures he found in the human body. He concluded that 'Galen described (I shall not say, imposed on us) the anatomy of the ape rather than of man, although the former differs in structure from the latter in many parts'.[8] The frontispiece of his *De Humani Corporis Fabrica* (*On the Structure of the Human Body*), published in 1543, shows Vesalius giving a practical anatomy lesson in an early medical theatre. Below the table bearing the foreshortened cadaver (the foreshortening on the part of the artist is another example of Renaissance empiricism), the barbers, dispossessed of their traditional employment, fiddle disconsolately with their razors. Now, when surgeons are regarded as the aristocrats or high priests of the medical profession, the disdain in which their steady-handed, delicate craft was once held seems extraordinary. But the revolution which Vesalius effected upon medicine was typical of several in an age which began to regard practical experience as the necessary foundation of theory.

The word *anatomy* was one of a number of imports (in this case from French) naturalised into English during the sixteenth century.[9] Its meaning of opening out to the view, displaying, separating and itemising the component parts of a body was suggestive in spheres other than the medical. It became an enormously fashionable word appearing in book titles (*The Anatomy of Sinne*, 1603; *An Anatomie of the World*, 1625; *The Anatomy of Warre*, 1642) in a way which suggests the desire of writers to authenticate their most abstract speculations with the idea of the demonstrable and visible. 'Let them anatomize Regan. See what breeds about her heart' (*King Lear*, III.vi.80). Shakespeare's King Lear, baffled and banished by his cruel daughters, finds in the metaphor of anatomy a good vehicle for his hurt rage: it suggests 'let them cut her up' as well as 'let us understand her'. Shakespeare's use of 'anatomize' here demonstrates the rapidity with which new words from areas of physical discovery could be assimilated and applied to the moral world. The way in which the physical could extend the moral – and vice versa – is demonstrated in

A. VESALII
OPERA OMNIA
ANATOMICA & CHIRVRGICA.
MDC CXXV.

gduni Batavorum Apud

Ldu Vivie et J. & H. Verbeek.

10.2. Frontispiece to
Andreas Vesalius,
Opera Omnia. This
plate had also been used
for the frontispiece of
*De Humani Corporis
Fabrica*

10.3. An illustration
from Thomas Geminus'
Compendiosa

what is perhaps the first pop-up anatomy picture in the 1559 edition of Thomas Geminus' *Compendiosa*.[10] The first plate of this work portrays two naked seated figures, a man and a woman. The woman carries a mirror bearing the inscription *Nosce Teipsum – Know Thyself*: a medieval moral one might think until lifting her belly one discovers beautifully layered cut-outs of the viscera inside.

The interested and eager assimilation of new words at this time is symptomatic of the excitement generated by the new worlds which both demanded and provided more words. The unequalled power and suggestiveness of the language of this period – during which Kyd, Marlowe, Shakespeare, Spenser, Jonson, Donne, Herbert, Marvell and Milton wrote – derives from the way in which words and the world beyond words were felt to be connected. The first dictionaries emerged at this time. The titles of some of them – John Florio's English-Italian *A Worlde of Wordes* (1598) and Edward Phillips' English-English *New World of English Words* (1658)[11] – suggest the felt continuity between the discoveries of language and those of the voyagers. The proliferation of words was an index of a proliferation of *knowledge*. When the speaker in John Donne's love poem says, 'Let sea-discoverers to new worlds have gone, / Let Maps to other, worlds on worlds have showne, / Let us possesse one world, each hath one, and is one' ('The good-morrow'), we feel that the new worlds discoverable by voyage or map have invigorated and extended the lovers' appreciation of the smaller worlds of their selves.

The new world of words was itself the object of much active interest. The acquisitiveness and nationalism of the Elizabethans were consciously extended to matters of language.[12] Literary translation was considered an act of patriotism. There were those who, like Sir Thomas Elyot, practised and championed a deliberate policy of coining new English words from Latin and Greek roots in order to 'bring the lernynges and wisedomes of them both in to this realme of England'.[13] Others, more purist in their nationalism, sought the coining of new words from exclusively English roots. Such a one was the philologist Sir John Cheke, Cambridge University's first Regius Professor of Greek. Cheke objected to the number of foreign-derived words used in existing translations of the Bible and he retaliated with his own version of Matthew's gospel in which 'moond', 'crossd' and 'hunderder', to give just three examples, translate Greek words which the King James Bible was to render as 'lunatike', 'crucified' and 'centurion'.[14] Such a policy, impossible to carry out systematically and comprehensibly, was also that of the nineteenth-century Dorset poet William Barnes who preferred 'sky-sill' to 'horizon'.

Neither Cheke nor Barnes had much influence on the course of the language which, thriving on impurity, expands and develops with little regard to those who would prescribe its course. But the controversy between those who, like Elyot, favoured the so-called 'ink-horn' or 'ink-pot' terms coined from foreign roots, and nationalistic purists like Cheke is an index of the serious attention which was applied to matters of linguistic expansion. Real or apparent archaism – the use of medieval-seeming words such as 'doughty', 'dight', 'eftsoones', 'whilome' – can offer another route for linguistic nationalism. According to Ben Jonson, the poet Edmund Spenser 'writ no Language' in 'affecting the Ancients' as he did.[15] Yet the deliberately archaic, pseudo-medieval language of Spenser's *Faerie Queene* (1596) directs its readers, not only to think about Britain's past, but to think more consciously about the way in which history informs language and the way in which the spelling of a word can sharpen our sense of its meaning by bringing out its origins.

The schoolmaster Holofernes in Shakespeare's *Love's Labour's Lost* is a great and absurd user of inkhornisms (such as 'peregrinate', from the Latin *peregrinare*, to travel), and he is also concerned that a word should display its origins in its pronunciation. He hates 'such rackers of orthography, as to speak dout, fine, when he should say dou*b*t; det, when he should pronounce de*b*t, – d, e, b, t;' (V.i.19ff.). During the sixteenth century spelling was very variable and flexible. The same word may be spelt in a variety of ways within a single text, and even proper names (such as Shake-Speare, Shakspere) lacked any stability when it came to spelling. The uniformity of typeface threw this variability into sharper relief and must have prompted the calls for a standardised spelling which began to be heard towards the end of the century. The argument was basically between etymology and phonetics: whether – as Holofernes would wish – our pronunciation should be determined by an etymologically-revealing spelling, or whether our spelling should reflect pronunciation (as Italian spelling does). The problem with the latter course is that pronunciation varies, but there were strong and effective moves to do away with some unsounded letters, such as inaudible final *e*s. And it is thanks to pedantry rather more thoughtful than Holofernes' that we now pronounce 'adventure' as we do, and not, as the French, *aventure*, and that we say 'perfect' (derived from the Latin, *perfectus*) and not, as before, 'parfit'.

The regulation of our language – our grammar, our spelling, our ideas about correct and incorrect use – is, like the British constitution, something that has been arrived at by practice and consensus. We have no officially appointed guardians of the language in the way that the French have in the *Académie Française* (founded in 1634) and the Italians in the *Accademia della Crusca* (founded in 1582). During the eighteenth century grammarians did their (often contradictory) best to prescribe what was permissible, but for Philip Sidney, writing in the 1590s, it is the eclecticism and grammatical fluidity of English which are the source of its expressive strength:

> some will say it is a mingled language. And why not so much the better, taking the best of both the other? Another will say it wanteth grammar. Nay truly, it hath that praise, that it wants not grammar ... being so easy in itself, and so void of those cumbersome differences of cases, genders, moods and tenses, which I think was a piece of the Tower of Babylon's curse, that a man should be put to school to learn his mother-tongue.[16]

But there were languages to be learned. The fascination with language extended to an increased awareness of the varieties of English spoken within Britain. And not only English: the first Welsh-English dictionary, compiled by William Salesbury in 1547 in response to Henry's edict that 'there shal hereafter be no difference in lawes and language btwyxte [the] subiectes of [the] princpalytye of Wales and [the] other subiects of [the] Royalme of Englande', was rapidly followed up by a key to the pronunciation of Welsh so that English speakers could use the dictionary to acquire the Welsh which was not dying out as the government had planned.[17]

Shakespeare represents Henry v's education in kingship as a process of language-learning. Prince Hal, before he becomes fit to govern and unite the divergent realm of England, sets himself an apprenticeship of acquiring the various tongues of his people. After a bout of calculated slumming, he prides himself on his command of low London idiom: 'They call drinking deep "dyeing scarlet", and when you breathe in your watering they cry '"Hem!" and bid you "Play it off!" To conclude, I am so good a proficient in one quarter of an hour that I can drink with any tinker in his own language during my life' (*Henry iv part I*, II.iv.15ff). Hal and Falstaff vye with each other to produce the most expressive similes:

> *Falstaff*: ... 'Sblood, I am as melancholy as a gib cat, or a lugged bear.
> *Prince*: Or an old lion, or a lover's lute.
> *Falstaff*: Yea, or the drone of a Lincolnshire bagpipe.
> *Prince*: What sayest thou to a hare, or the melancholy of Moor-ditch?
> *Falstaff*: Thou hast the most unsavoury similes, and art indeed the most comparative rascalliest sweet young prince.
>
> (I.ii.71ff)

That ability to be 'comparative', finding metaphorical connections between disparate experiences, is one which today we tend to think the province of poetry. Added to this is the widely held belief that poetry is icing on the cake, not 'serious'. But until the latter part of the seventeenth century the principle of analogy was used as an instrument of discovery: an opportunity for multiplying and processing information about the world. It is probably still true that the great leaping perceptions of scientific discovery are akin to the revelations and intuitions of poetry. But orthodox procedure does not cater for such exceptions. The sciences have themselves multiplied into disciplines with highly specialised and technical languages which lack the inbuilt possibility of discovery and connection which a common language provides. But in the sixteenth and seventeenth centuries, at the time when experimental science was taking off, the language in which discoveries were recorded and the language which enabled discoveries to be made, was the shared language of common speech – stretched, modified, but still basically the common language.

The technological development of lock gates enabled William Harvey to understand the principle of coronary valves. The perception of this analogy enabled him to see the possibility, and thence the reality, of the circulation of the blood. Harvey's work is full of metaphor: not out of any striving to be poetic but because it seeks to explain new concepts in a language understandable by all. The arteries, he writes, 'are fill'd like Satchells or baggs [rather than] blown up like bladders'. He writes of the 'streyner of the lungs' and concludes that:

> it was necessary that the heart should receive the blood continually into the ventricles, as in a pond or cistern, and send it forth again: and for this reason it was necessary that it should be serv'd with four locks or doors, whereof two should serve for the intromission and two for the emission of blood.[18]

For Francis Bacon, whose work represents the last sane attempt by one individual to address the totality of human knowledge, 'whatever deserves to exist deserves also to be known'.[19] This fearless open-mindedness is accompanied by an assurance that what is knowable is also sayable and that the language is, to quote Sidney again, 'capable of any excellent exercising of it'.[20] The language available to (and extended by) Shakespeare, the language available to the committee of forty-seven men appointed by James I to translate the Bible and whose aim was 'that it may be understood even of the very vulgar',[21] was the common language that had been stretched, enriched and validated by a wealth of new information. There are those who, in an evasive modern way, read the King James Bible 'for its prose' as if its language were not concerned with matter. Indeed it is remarkable how many of the writers of the seventeenth century currently valued for their prose were not primarily concerned with producing works of 'literature', that special category in which good writing is now stowed: writers such as Francis Bacon, Thomas Browne, Richard Hooker, Thomas Hobbes – scientists, theologians, philosophers – writing at a time when good thinking and good knowing quite clearly meant good saying.

But Thomas Hobbes, working in the latter part of the seventeenth century, was deeply distrustful of the language he used so forcefully. 'Words are wise men's counters, they do but reckon by them: but they are the mony of fooles'.[22] He, and others of his generation, found the common language too volatile, too metaphorically charged, too suggestive for philosophical exposition. They looked to the mute vocabulary of mathematical signs for a greater security. The formation of the Royal Society in 1662 marks the beginning of our modern era of specialisation with its corresponding multiplication of specialised (and often non-verbal) languages. Logic itself, though derived from the Greek word for 'word', *logos*, is now accomplished with mathematical symbols.

The English language at the end of the sixteenth and beginning of the seventeenth centuries was at its fullest and most expressive stretch as bearer and instrument of knowledge. But it is as if it stretched itself to breaking point for, by the end of the seventeenth century, the common English language was ceasing to be the language common to all branches of learning, all areas of experience. The dictionaries and spelling reforms of the sixteenth century reflect an atmosphere of charged excitement about language, but they also mark the beginning of an urge towards classification which reached its peak during the eighteenth century. *The Essay Towards a Real Character* (1668) of John Wilkins, first Secretary of the Royal Society, represents a somewhat desperate attempt to limit the proliferation and undo the arbitrariness of words by an extraordinarily elaborate system of classifying objects and qualities, each with a corresponding sign. In his version of the Creed, for example, the sign ∠‾‾‾‾‾ denotes God the Father. Wilkins explains that 'a streight Line being the most simple, is put for the Character of God. The acute angle on the left side doth denote the first person of the Blessed Trinity, namely *God the Father*'.[23]

One cannot read Wilkins 'for his prose'. His system of signification is oppressed and vitiated by its refusal to concede that the categories which it would subserve are themselves partly verbal creations. Literary and non-literarary language were becoming increasingly distinct and, though the English language was spoken and read by more people than ever before – in the British Isles, in North America and the West Indies – a knowledge of it could no longer offer an entry into all other available forms of knowledge. It was to an earlier period that Samuel Johnson looked when compiling his great dictionary, issued in 1755:

> From the authours which rose in the time of *Elizabeth*, a speech might be formed adequate to all the purposes of use and elegance. If the language of theology were extracted from *Hooker* and the translation of the Bible; the terms of natural knowledge from *Bacon*; the phrases of policy, war, and navigation from *Raleigh*, the dialect of poetry and fiction from *Spenser* and *Sidney*; and the diction of common life from *Shakespeare*, few ideas would be lost to mankind, for want of *English* words, in which they might be expressed.[24]

Further reading

R.S. Jones, *The Triumph of the English Language* (Stanford, 1953); Louis B. Wright, *Middle Class Culture in Elizabethan England* (Chapel Hill, 1935); G.D. Willcock, *Shakespeare as a Critic of Language* (London, 1934); F.O. Mathiesen, *Translation: an Elizabethan Art* (Cambridge, Mass., 1931); Henry Bradley, *The Making of English* (London, 1968); F.F. Bruce, *The English Bible* (London, 1970); C. Hill, *Intellectual Origins of the English Revolution* (Oxford, 1965); D.T. Starnes and G.E. Noyes, *The English Dictionary from Cawdrey to Johnson* (Chapel Hill, 1946).

PLVRA · LATEN°T · QVAM · PATENT

GENERAL AND RARE MEMORIALS
pertayning to the Perfect Arte of
NAVIGATION:
Annexed to the PARADOXAL *Cumpas, in Playne :*
now firſt publiſhed : 24. yeres, after the firſt
Inuention thereof.

ΙΕΡΟΓΛΥΦΙΚΟΝ

ΒΡΥΤΑΝΙΚΟΝ

Trade and Territory
The Rise of Imperial Britain 1603–1763

Bruce Lenman

Most of us assume that the British empire was a creation of Queen Elizabeth I. The vision of an imperial sovereign surrounded by her sea dogs is seductive. It goes back to the political propaganda put out during the great queen's lifetime in the shape of symbolic portraits like the 'Armada Portrait' which depicts her in 1588 at the height of her triumph over Philip II of Spain's 'Felicissima Armada' (the Happy or Most Fortunate Fleet whose fate in that year so much belied its optimistic name). Other portraits of Elizabeth are full of maritime and imperial symbolism. Her poets saluted her as 'Astrea', the imperial virgin from classical mythology whose reign was destined to bring an era of peace and fruitfulness to the earth. How far did reality match all this propaganda, churned out by a regime which was almost always insecure?

For a start, it must be stressed that if the British empire has a parent it is that canny Scot, James VI, who united the British Isles under his sceptre in 1603. Not all his subjects agreed with his characteristically modest theory that this union was part of God's plan for mankind's salvation, nor were they very co-operative in pushing forward with schemes of political integration. James nevertheless assumed the title of king of Great Britain to symbolise the birth of a new European great power.[1]

Elizabeth's Tudor state complex consisted only of the two linked kingdoms of England and Ireland. Both were what was left of a French-speaking colonial empire in the British Isles. They dated back

11.1. Elizabeth I portrayed as mistress of the known world

11.2. Elizabeth I: the Armada portrait

to the Norman conquest of England in 1066, and the erection of the lordship of Ireland by the Angevin Henry II in 1171. In theory, both were unitary colonial jurisdictions subject to one Common Law, but the Irish state became incapable of governing anything except a small strip of territory round its capital of Dublin. Beyond this Pale lived independent Gaelic princes opposed to any central rule, especially if alien. Henry VIII, Elizabeth's father, had proclaimed himself king of Ireland in 1540, but he did not extend the reach of his Irish administration.[2] Paradoxically, all that was left of the original continental imperial heartland of Normandy was the small archipelago of the Channel Islands, where Elizabeth ruled as duke.

The central political institution of these several realms was the royal court. Sir Walter Raleigh, Captain of its Royal Guard, was a pioneer of English settlement in America. As early as 1578 his half-brother Sir Humphrey Gilbert obtained a royal patent for six years authorising him to take possession of 'any remote barbarous and heathen lands not possessed by any Christian prince or people'. Raleigh soldiered in Ireland where in 1586 he received a grant of 40,000 acres of forfeited Desmond lands on the Blackwater, and between 1600 and 1603 he served as governor of Jersey, a job to which he devoted much time.[3] Elizabeth's biggest territorial achievement was the conquest of Ireland. James came to England in time to receive the surrender of the last great Ulster rebel, Hugh O'Neill, second earl of Tyrone.

Richard Eden had been the first to translate the accounts of the Spanish and Italian voyages into English. In 1553 he published *A Treatyse of the Newe India*, extracted and translated from a French edition of Sebastian Münster's *Cosmographia: Beschreibung aller Lender*, published in Basel in 1544. With the accession of Mary Tudor and her marriage to Philip of Spain he was inspired to translate the work of Peter Martyr, 'Cheife Secretary to the Emperour Charles the fift, and of his Privie Councell', an early official chronicler of Spanish expansion in the New World. Even with Philip as king of England and Ireland by matrimonial right, Eden was as anxious to display a field of opportunity as he was to flatter Spaniards. After the accession of the Protestant Elizabeth in 1558, the marginal notes to Eden's translations, which originated in manuscript marginalia in his own original copies, became or were made by later editors (he died in 1576) distinctly anti-papist. These translations preceded by forty years the better-known compilation of Richard Hakluyt, *The principall navigations, voiages and discoveries of the English nation*, published first in London in 1589. Richard Hakluyt the Younger was an Anglican clergyman who like his lawyer cousin and namesake was an advocate of English overseas expansion. In 1582 he published a short collection of narratives of voyages, designed to establish English primacy in the discovery of North America.[5] In July 1584 he left his chaplaincy to the English ambassador in Paris to consult with Raleigh in London and to pen a confidential state memorandum known as the 'Discourse of Western Planting'. It argued that English colonies in North America would provide valuable raw materials; act as markets for English goods; and provide bases for attacks on Spanish treasure fleets and Spanish and Portuguese fishermen. Portugal had become one of the kingdoms of Philip II in 1580.[6]

Another propagandist for overseas expansion was the Welsh mathematician and astrologer John Dee. He advocated an 'Imperial Thalassocracy', a 'British Impire' in high latitudes based on maritime commerce and naval power. Apart from the voyages by John and Sebastian Cabot out of Bristol in the late fifteenth and early sixteenth centuries, he based Queen Elizabeth's right to rule North America on the mythical explorations of the Welsh prince Owen Madoc in the twelfth century. His ideas were as unrealistic as the frontispiece to one of his books published in 1577 which showed his patron Queen Elizabeth as Mistress of the Seas.[7]

Between 1584 and 1588 Sir Walter Raleigh sponsored a series of attempts to establish an English colony on Roanoke island at the mouth of Albemarle Sound, just south of the Chesapeake. His cousin Sir Richard Grenville sailed out of Plymouth with the first party of settlers on 9 April 1585. Raleigh's Virginia aborted for several reasons, but mainly because the costly and difficult operation of setting up a community in a distant unknown land was beyond the financial resources of a single person.[8] Piracy, as even the Virginia settlers found, did pay. Elizabethan England, waging open naval war against Spain from 1584, made a rational decision to put its assets into the profitable business of piracy against Spanish and Portuguese shipping in the Atlantic and Caribbean, rather than into the profitless ploy of settlement colonies. Piracy boomed right up to 1603 when the accession of King James, followed by the conclusion of Anglo-Spanish peace by the Treaty of London of 1604, endangered the industry. King James hated pirates, and since he could deprive them of most of their bases, they had to find other occupations.[9]

Compared with the repeated failures in North American colonisation, Elizabethan trade with the Orient proved profitable. On the last day of 1600 a charter was granted to 'the Governor and Company of Merchants of London trading into the East Indies'. The London

11.3. The Farrer map, showing how early settlers envisaged America

merchant Ralph Fitch had in 1591 returned from a journey to Goa, the Deccan, Bengal, Burma, Malacca and Ceylon,[10] but the real reason for the formation of the East India Company was the success of a series of Dutch voyages to the Spice Islands of Indonesia. Sir James Lancaster, who commanded the two first English voyages to the East Indies, sailed on the first in 1591. It was a fiasco, ending with shipwreck in the West Indies. Lancaster recovered his losses by leading a successful pirate raid on the Portuguese harbour of Pernambuco in Brazil in 1594, where he captured 'a rich East Indian carack – together with great abundance of sugars, Brasil-wood, and cotton'. In 1600 he commanded the successful first voyage by the East India Company.[11] After 1604, several London entrepreneurs who had invested heavily in privateering in American waters prudently redirected their money into the East India Company. Many men in the Jacobean era were interested in both that company and American colonisation. Richard Hakluyt looked after the company archives from 1600 to his death in 1616. Thomas Andrews, one of the leading London puritan merchants who backed the establishment of Plymouth Colony by the Pilgrim Fathers after 1620, was also governor of the East India Company.

The East India trade was unpopular with some writers because it consisted mainly of the export of British bullion to the East where it was exchanged for spices, textiles and luxury goods. Import-led growth always worried moralists. However, it paid. In their early stages, American colonies did not. The London merchants who invested in the original company which sponsored the move of the Pilgrim Fathers from Leyden to New England lost most of their money, though the businessmen who later supplied essential goods at high prices and interest to the struggling colony did well.[12] It was the Great Puritan Migration which finally established New England as a significant colony. Between 1630 and 1640 approximately 20,000 people moved into the region to escape from the unpopular political and religious policies of King Charles I and Archbishop Laud. They were part of a total of about 65,000 English people who migrated to North America and the West Indies in this period. The fading away of immigration after 1640 removed a positive stimulus in the emergent New England economy, precipitating a crisis which local merchants only gradually solved. Prosperity for the region came to depend more on the sea, where fishing and opportunities for merchant shipping flourished, than on land.[13]

Further south, an expedition from London had in 1607 made a start both to the continuous history of Virginia, and to an English empire of settlement in North America when it established a community at Jamestown, thirty miles above Hampton Roads on Chesapeake Bay.

The site was an appallingly unhealthy one. Mortality rates were crippling, and the costs of sustaining not very adaptable settlers in the face of food shortages and Indian attacks like the massacre of 1622, which cost 350 settler lives in one day, drove the sponsoring Virginia Company into bankruptcy. The fact that a joint stock company was prepared to spend far more money than Sir Walter Raleigh expended on Virginia saved the colony, if not the company. Though there were always optimists who hoped to develop a silk industry, find gold mines, or reach the Pacific (with its promise of trade with China) just beyond the headwaters of the James River, the colony proved no bonanza. It was saved by a staple crop of which King James deeply disapproved – tobacco. Despite James's authorship of a *Counter-Blaste to Tobacco*, the Chesapeake colony was, as Charles i remarked in 1627, 'wholly built upon smoke'. It had no option other than tobacco. There was no great native empire to rape, as the Spaniards had raped the Aztec and Inca empires. Settlement had to be made to pay by means of a profitable crop, and tobacco was that crop. Where it grew, settlement grew. In 1632, Charles granted Cecilius Calvert, Lord Baltimore, the proprietary charter which marked the birth of the colony of Maryland. It was a refuge for Roman Catholic dissenters, but also another Chesapeake colony.

After 1660 there was further extensive developent under Charles ii, who cancelled an unpaid debt to Admiral Sir William Penn by means of a vast proprietary grant on the west bank of the River Delaware to the Quaker son and namesake of the sailor. Pennsylvania's growth was matched by the development of the Carolinas to the south of Virginia, and in 1664 the gap in the English seaboard colonies was filled when the Dutch colony of New Netherlands was seized and renamed New York for the heir to the British thrones, James, duke of York. These colonies differed widely. In New England there were few slaves, and settlers soon had remarkably good life expectancy. The Chesapeake colonies were places where a twenty-year-old colonist was statistically likely to die in his early forties. Before 1700 the Chesapeake populations were incapable of reproducing themselves, and survived due to heavy immigration. White bond servants, who exchanged their liberty for a fixed term of years for a passage across the Atlantic, provided originally the bulk of the field hands. They were recruited by commercial agents, usually in English ports. In America they produced staples like tobacco and the grain which the Chesapeake colonies exported to England's West Indian colonies. The Somers or Bermuda Isles, nearly 600 miles due east of South Carolina, had been settled as early as 1612. Thereafter English seamen explored the Bahamas and between 1604 and 1640 established significant colonies on five islands of the Lesser Antilles – Barbados, St Christopher,

Nevis, Antigua and Monserrat. In 1655, as part of Oliver Cromwell's 'Western Design', Jamaica was seized from Spain.

Originally, these sea islands were meant to be settled by white freeholders who would provide manpower for defence. The first governor of Jamaica, General William Brayne, came directly from commanding the Cromwellian fort at Inverlochy in the highlands of Scotland, where his job had been to hold down the western clans. In practice the island colonies rapidly became specialist sugar-producers, using black slaves as their work force. Already the Portuguese and Dutch had established a vast Atlantic trade in replacing the disease-ravaged native American populations by robust African slaves. Jamestown had bought a few black slaves from a Dutch ship as early as 1619, but it was towards the end of the century that black slaves became the predominant field workers of the Chesapeake region.[14] A rise in living standards in England, and degradation of manual work by association with slavery, discouraged recruitment of white bond servants. 'No taxation without representation' was a phrase coined in Barbados. It had more of a future in Virginia where assertive white settlers were not reduced to a tiny minority in a sea of unfree blacks.

In the Far East the last thing the English East India Company wanted was territorial dominion. In India it had made early contact with the Mughal emperor who dominated the northern plains and who was expanding southwards into the Deccan. Captain William Hawkins, whose ship reached Surat in 1608, had proceeded from there to the imperial court at Agra where his ability to speak Turkish made him acceptable to the emperor Jahangir, head of a Turkish-speaking dynasty originally from Central Asia. Between 1615 and 1619 King James IV and I had an ambassador, the experienced diplomat Sir Thomas Roe, accredited to Jahangir. 'Profit, not grandeur, which is our end in trading', was a constant company theme. Roe entirely agreed. He argued that: 'It is the beggering of the Portugall, notwithtanding his many rich residences and territoryes, that he keepes souldiers that spendes it.' He went on to say:

> He never Profited by the Indyes, since he defended them. Observe this well. It hath been also the error of the Dutch, who seeke Plantation heere by the Swoord – it is an error to affect Garrisons and Land warrs in India.[15]

Even Roe was prepared to use force at sea against anyone trying to obstruct company trade. By the 1680s the East India Company had resigned itself to the necessity of fortifying its principal factories or trading stations in India to protect them from the effects of local anarchy. That they then became havens for Indian merchants and an

11.4. Emperor Jahangir
with James VI/I

implicit challenge to traditional authority was a paradoxical result.[16]

It was a platitude of seventeenth-century discourse that 'There is no Profit without Power'. Seventeenth-century Englishmen were prepared to use the power of the state both as a regulatory force, and as an aggressive war machine. Under the republican regime of the Commonwealth and Protectorate the combination of parliamentary regulation of trade, and the might of the British navy, became formidable. Lord Protector Oliver Cromwell ruled a Commonwealth which united England, Scotland, Ireland and their associated territories, and which built 147 new warships between 1649 and 1654. Its arch-rival in trade was the Republic of the United Netherlands. Rivalry with the Dutch in the Orient was of long-standing. In 1623 the Dutch had massacred British settlers on the clove island of Amboina in the Moluccas, on a trumped-up charge of involvement in a native revolt. The English East India Company turned away from the Spice Islands to India, but it nursed its grievances. However, it was Dutch rivalry in the carrying trade which precipitated the Navigation Act of 9 October 1651, a measure aimed at taking the shipping of English goods out of the clutches of the Dutch.

The 'Mother Trade' of Dutch commerce was the enormous volume of business done by Dutch businessmen and shipowners with the countries of Northern Europe, and especially with the Baltic. Less plagued by piracy in northern waters than elsewhere, and regularly convoyed by specialist warships, Dutch vessels evolved into highly functional unarmed floating holds with sail plans operable by a minimum crew. They offered such cheap freights that they dominated much of the import-export trade in British harbours, and in the harbours of the English colonies. The Act of 1651 obliged importers to use ships belonging to Englishmen or to the actual producers of their imports. It confined the import trade of the colonies and the export trade thence to England entirely to English ships. With the conquest and integration of Scotland and Ireland, these countries were included within the definition of 'English', as always were the overseas plantations themselves. At the Restoration of the Stuarts in 1660 another Act confirmed the system, though its application was restricted to England proper and its overseas plantations. Indeed the 1660 Act of Navigation extended the system of controls to exports 'enumerating' colonial commodities such as tobacco, sugar, ginger, cotton and indigo, which might only be shipped to Europe through English ports. This *entrepôt* function was reinforced by the Staple Act of 1663 which required the despatch of European goods to the plantations via English ports. When the fiscal demands of war led to a sharp rise in English tariffs, and Scotland was admitted into the structure by the Union of 1707, there emerged a serious attempt to

create a self-sufficient Atlantic superpower. Of course, reality and
theory never matched. Smuggling was common. In the bulk carrying
trades, especially with Scandinavia, English shipping was never fully
adequate. In North America, Virginia paid some attention to the
statutes, but New England virtually ignored them, while for a long
period the West Indian colonies had to be licensed to deal with the
Dutch.[17]

Yet the same period saw three great wars of maritime aggression
against the Dutch. Of these the most successful by far was the one
waged in 1652–4 by the republican regime, urged on by London
commercial interests. Exploiting a strategic position athwart Dutch
trade routes, the British navy made huge captures of Dutch merchant
shipping. Cromwell disliked the war, ended it as soon as he decently
could, and turned with relief against Spain.

After the Restoration the heir presumptive to the British thrones,
the duke of York, with his Roman Catholic and absolutist tastes, led
the attack on the republican and Protestant rulers of the Netherlands.
The second Anglo-Dutch war of 1665–7 failed to produce the
expected easy victories and ended in fiasco as Admiral de Ruyter
destroyed the fleet of Charles II in the Medway. The third Anglo-
Dutch war of 1672–4 was fought in alliance with France. It was
unpopular from the start. The Treaty of Breda of 1674 which put
Charles II out of the war contained nominal concessions designed to
save his face, and the Dutch had to return the New York they
recaptured in 1673, but in substance Dutch skill and heroism fought
off Stuart imperialism.[18] By 1674 most British people thought that
their most dangerous potential enemy was not the Dutch Republic but
the absolutist, Catholic, military monarchy of Louis XIV's France.
Louis' great minister Colbert had embarked on the construction of a
powerful battle fleet. When in 1677 the head of the Stuart naval
administration, Samuel Pepys, appeared before the English House of
Commons to appeal, in his capacity as 'Secretary to the office of Lord
High Admiral of England', for funds to built thirty new ships of war,
he had to acknowledge the reality of this new threat. He appealed for
support against both the greedy Dutch and the imperious French.[19]

The Restoration saw the emergence of a truly imperial Britain.
Economically, it rested on the plantation production of tropical or
semi-tropical staples such as sugar, rice, tobacco and indigo. White
settlers and black slaves moved westwards across the Atlantic to feed
worker-hungry colonies. Even in the far north, the Hudson's Bay
Company, chartered by Charles II in 1670 with the dashing Prince
Rupert as its first governor, pressed on the northern limits of French
Canada as it strove to maximise its share of the 150,000 beaver pelts
which Canada could in a good year send to Europe. In the Orient the

11.5. Charles II's charter to the Hudson Bay Company

East India Company continued to seek profit rather than dominion. Its trade expanded spectacularly, and in 1668 Charles II transferred to it the port of Bombay for a nominal rent of £10 per annum. He thereby rid himslf of a burden acquired as part of the dowry of his Portuguese bride of 1662, Catherine of Braganza.

What imperial Britain lacked was political coherence. In Massachusetts writs did not even run in the name of the king until after 1660. In 1676 a turning point came when significant royal naval and military forces had to be sent to put down Bacon's Rebellion in Virginia. This was a frontier rebellion against the local oligarchy, and was precipitated by the failure of the leader of the oligarchy, Governor Sir William Berkeley, to respond effectively to Indian attacks on the settlers. The Stuarts moved in on colony after colony to assert their imperial monarchy.[20] Because they were locked in a vicious struggle with the king's parliament of England, over the right of York to succeed his brother, they in no way based their authority on that

particular legislature. They were happy to recognise regional legis-
latures, in their place. The mature imperialism of James II and VII after
1685 moved towards a coherent pattern for imperial Britain. It was to
be a series of co-equal kingdoms held together by the crown and its
servants, civil and military. The three kingdoms of the home
archipelago – England, Scotland and Ireland – were to be balanced by
northern and southern American Dominions of which one, the
Dominion of New England with Sir Edmund Andros as governor
general, was actually set up.[21]

The whole structure disintegrated when the Glorious Revolution of
1688 overthrew James in England. A series of upheavals followed in
every other part of the British world, as was inevitable when William
of Orange so successfully seized control of the core kingdom. The
much-hated Dominion of New England disintegrated. There was a
rather radical revolution in Scotland, and a bloody civil war in Ireland
which laid the foundations of the eighteenth-century Protestant
Ascendancy. Not only was the 1688 Revolution different in nature in
each separate part of the British world, but it was also subject to
radically different interpretations. The extremes of interpretation were
to be found everywhere: what mattered was the version accepted by
the wielders of social and political power at local level.

In England the consensus was always very conservative. To carry
Anglican Tories with their doctrines of passive obedience and divine
right along with them, the Whigs, who were the activists in the
Glorious Revolution, had to agree to the preposterous official theory
that James had 'abdicated'. James himself was clear he had been
deposed by rebels and heretics. Official England came to decline to say
what the 'Revolution Principles' on which its government rested were.
Equally, official England disliked too nice a definition of 'English
liberties'. As for concepts such as representation, or problems such as
the relationship between government and governed, the less said the
better. In practice, the Westminster parliament of king, Lords and
Commons assumed the absolutist pretensions of late Stuart monarchy.
The economically and politically privileged classes of England, and
after 1707 Great Britain, had as a safeguard their own two-thirds
share in the new absolute sovereign.[22] It was hardly surprising that
many individuals associated with the government of James II survived
to serve William III.

Among them was the arch-imperial 'fixer' William Blathwayt, who
more than any other English civil servant tried to co-ordinate the
Atlantic state complex. His central obsession was that of his royal
master King William – the cycle of wars with France which occupied
most of the period 1688–1713. By the end of those wars Captain
Southack RN was so convinced of the French threat to British North

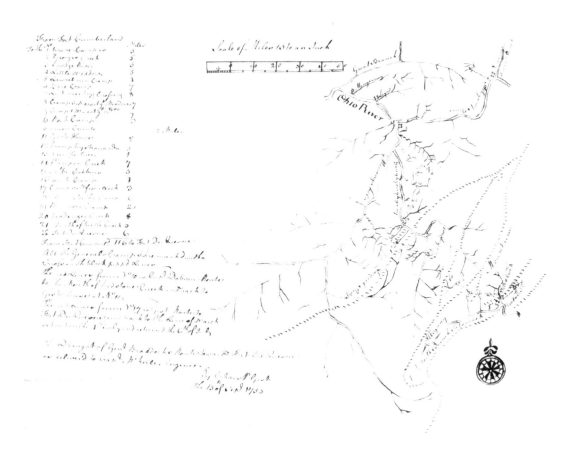

11.6. General
Braddock's journey in
1755

America that in 1717 he published a map to illustrate it. From Quebec
a slender chain of French forts and settlements stretched through lakes
Ontario and Erie, down the rivers Ohio and Mississippi, and linked
up with the French territory of Louisiana around New Orleans. In
confused warfare with the Bourbon powers of Spain and France
between 1739 and 1748 the British government was lucky to emerge
with no great losses of territory.

It was the sensational run of imperial victories in the 1750s under
the leadership of the elder William Pitt which really brought problems
to a head. In 1757 Robert Clive seized a great territorial empire in
India in Bengal and Bihar at the battle of Plassey. The Peace of Paris in
1763 not only confirmed British gains in West Africa and the West
Indies, but also confirmed the expulsion of France from Canada. But
there was a worm in the bud, because then, as now, the whole concept
of being British was full of unresolved ambiguity. Wherein lay the
ultimate sovereignty in the British world? Was not the very concept of
ultimate sovereignty a dangerous and mischievous one? Were the
Americans truly British? They insisted that they were Englishmen as

well as Americans. They asserted that they had taken the inalienable Rights and Liberties of Englishmen with them to the New World. American colonists held a radical view of Revolution Principles and had learned from English opposition writers to suspect that there was a plot by Westminster to take liberties – theirs.[23]

Sir Josiah Child had argued before 1700 that an empire of white settlement in America would breed political opposition to the authoritarian government he liked. He would have preferred an empire of conquest in India, but he botched an attempt to conquer Bengal in 1687–90. By 1779 King George III was being depicted as a 'Botching Taylor' whose empire was in shreds due to the American Revolution.[24] Imperial triumphs in 1763 proved a prelude to disaster. Westminster politicians claimed an absolute sovereignty over the British world which they never had and could not enforce. Frightened by the size of their war debts after 1763, they tried to tax the Americans, who resisted. The flight of Liberty to America became a platitude.[25] By 1775 a great civil war had broken out in the Atlantic-divided English nation. Imperial triumph had brought out the underlying political failure. When, in 1774, Boston radicals precipitated the final crisis by dumping English East India Company tea in the harbour, that political failure at the heart of imperial Britain was plain for all to see.[26]

Further reading

Kenneth R. Andrews, *Trade, Plunder and Settlement: Maritime Enterprise and the Genesis of the British Empire, 1480–1630* (Cambridge, 1984); D.B. Quinn and A.N. Ryan, *England's Sea Empire 1550–1642* (London, 1983); Stephen Saunders Webb, *The Governors-General: The English Army and the Definition of Empire, 1569–1681* (Chapel Hill, 1979); K.N. Chaudhuri, *Trade and Civilisation in the Indian Ocean: An Economic History from the Rise of Islam to 1750* (Cambridge, 1985); Ralph Davis, *The Rise of the Atlantic Economies* (London, 1973); Angus Calder, *Revolutionary Empire: The Rise of the English-speaking Empires from the fifteenth century to the 1780s* (London, 1981).

CHAPTER
TWELVE

Britain under Westminster

L.M. Cullen

In 1500, the British Isles consisted of one moderately strong kingdom, England, and two weak ones, Ireland and Scotland. The separate nations, England, Ireland, Scotland and we should add a separate Wales, were not only disunited but weak in comparison to the emerging unified powers of France and Spain. In 1763, the situation was entirely different. Britain had just established an empire that stretched westwards towards Canada and eastwards to India, largely wrested from the French. How did this transformation come about? More important, why did it occur during this period from 1500 to 1763?

There are two reasons for this. First of all, within this period the separate nations within the British Isles became subservient, formally or informally, to the direction of the government and parliament at Westminster. Alone, of course, this was not enough to transform Britain into a great power. But it was paralleled by a much more dramatic centralisation of resources – men and money alike – which gave the government of Britain in the eighteenth century the money and manpower to match on equal terms the greatest powers in Europe and create an empire.

England in 1500 was not exactly a weak country: the demands posed by innumerable wars to defend and ultimately lose the French lands that its Norman kings had brought with them gave it a political unity which Ireland and Scotland lacked. But in countless medieval wars England had not proved strong enough to wear down the Scots and Irish and had been forced to acquiesce in a decline in its stake in both kingdoms. The growth of a powerful France and Spain, however, raised the spectre of foreign interference in the affairs of Scotland or Ireland. The alliance of the Scots with the French from the 1540s to the 1560s, the presence of French troops, courtiers and even a regent,

Mary of Guise, and the marriage of her daughter, Mary, Queen of Scots, to the dauphin of France in 1558 all pointed to the dangers. In consequence, English monarchs no longer felt free to live with an uneasy compromise close to their own heartland.

Fears of subversion by France among the Scots and the Irish were turned into a still deeper anxiety by the new-found importance that the distant waters of the cold Atlantic were acquiring. As navigators from all the coastal countries of western Europe crossed the Atlantic and explored the islands and the mainland coast, rivalries were transferred from Europe.[1] Europeans accustomed to kill each other at home almost immediately began the same process in the new world. Thus traditional hostilities transformed themselves into rivalries at sea and in new lands. Indeed, overseas inhibitions were fewer than at home, and Englishmen found themselves in competition with Spaniards, Frenchmen and the Dutch. In particular, worsening relations in distant waters were a major factor in the growing distrust between Spain and England.

Deteriorating relations with European powers were matched by the vigour of English intervention in Scotland from the 1540s until 1560, when France was the main threat, or in Ireland from the 1570s to the 1590s, when the Spanish interest was the most menacing. From 1560, when French intervention in Scotland ended,[2] Ireland presented a greater danger. Moreover, the success of the Protestant reformers in Scotland in that decade meant that while the reformers in England and Scotland might be divided on the precise form of government the new church should have, Scotland no longer held out any hopes for the Catholic French. On the other hand, the Reformation did not take hold in Ireland, and the growing religious divide between the Catholic Irish and their Protestant English rulers reinforced the weakness of central government in Ireland by making the country tempting to England's enemies.[3]

The response to this challenge lay in a long-drawn-out effort by England to subjugate its neighbours Scotland and Ireland involving protracted war and negotiation; in the case of Wales, already conquered, union with England was made formal. Henry VIII, mere lord of Ireland, had himself declared king in 1541 for fear some foreign monarch might do so first. Relations with Scotland were made easier by the fact that through dynastic marriage links James VI of Scotland became James I of England. A complete union of the two kingdoms was one of his wishes, but his Scottish subjects would have nothing to do with the idea. Cromwell, who rode roughshod over most interests which confronted him, created a political union of the three kingdoms in the 1650s but, carried through without the consent of the Scots and Irish, this came to nought in the Restoration of the monarchy in 1660. Thus in 1660, the position in Britain was that while there was a sole monarchy for the three kingdoms, there were still three separate parliaments.

Although Scotland proved troublesome in the 1640s, it was Ireland that proved the biggest obstacle to British security after 1560. After 1534, England ceased to leave its administration and military campaigns in Ireland in the hands of local subjects, and English soldiers and administrators began to make the direct acquaintanceship of Irish conditions. Lack of interest was replaced by some degree of fascination with the people and land they were subjugating.[4] The writings and drawings of Elizabethans in Ireland depicted Irish society for the benefit of those at home. The sketches in John Derrick's *Image of Ireland*, in 1581, afford a glimpse of this world. Spencer's *Faerie Queen*, composed in praise of his queen, Elizabeth, was actually written while he was a colonist in County Cork. Military mappers at the end of the century give us a graphic picture of Elizabethan fortifications, of the houses and residences of their enemies and of the bogs, waste land and forest in which much of the war of attrition took place.[5]

The Elizabethan wars did not finish the struggle. In all, it took three major campaigns from the 1590s to 1691 to subjugate Ireland. Precisely because the country lacked the rudimentary political unity which Scotland enjoyed, provincial resistance seemed endless and shifting. In the culminating wars from 1689 to 1691, the forces of the Protestant king, William, faced not only the supporters of the deposed James II, but perhaps the most professional army ever to have landed in the British Isles, some 7000 troops of the French king, Louis XIV.[6] But despite this support, James was decisively defeated, and any prospect of further resistance in Ireland was crushed.

But what had secured Ireland, the crushing defeat of James II, raised the spectre of future troubles in Scotland. The only major support that James or the later Stuart pretenders could now summon was in the Scottish highlands. Memories of the toughness of the Scots were painful in London, and there was no doubt about the formidable nature of any Jacobite challenge which would command widespread support in Scotland. This fear explains why a full union between Scotland and England took place in 1707.[7] Uncertainty about the future accounted for England's readiness to offer terms attractive enough to overcome traditional Scottish doubts about union. So precisely because of the threat that the return of a pretender offered, the Scots not only pulled off a union in 1707, but one largely on their own terms. This helped to guarantee the loyalty of the lowland gentry, whose local managers under the union remained, moreover, Scotsmen, not Englishmen. The idea of union, once it was aired with Scotland,

12.1. Cartoon showing
the might of the
Republic of England
(1653)

was welcomed by the Irish Protestants as well. But it had no appeal
for the government in London. No threat was anticipated in Ireland.
Indeed, because the victory in 1691 had given the Irish Protestants a
new sense of confidence English officials found them remarkably
truculent. Their loyalty was not in doubt, but little benefit that
England did not already enjoy could be foreseen from the appearance
in Westminster of a group who, as events in Ireland had already
shown, were determined to take a narrow local view of their interests,
rather than the wider perspective befitting a monarch with interests
often in the Catholic courts of Europe.

But fears of rebellion in Scotland remained real, and rebellions or
invasions were attempted in 1708, 1715 and 1719.[8] Fears of this
highland threat were evident constantly in government policy towards
Scotland. A chain of forts was built across the highlands; General
Wade built his celebrated military roads in the glens, and the Black
Watch was created as a loyal force of highlanders to keep order in the
highlands and keep an eye on disloyal clansmen.[9] The threat
eventuated in 1745 when Bonnie Prince Charlie landed. Many rallied
in the highlands to his standard, and he was able to penetrate as far

12.2. The Irish host fires
an enemy's house (John
Derrick)

12.3. The English army
leaves Dublin Castle
(John Derrick)

12.4. The English and
Irish join battle (John
Derrick)

south as Derbyshire before his retreat and final rout on the bloody field of Culloden.

Britain's emergence as a great political power depended on more than the ability to fend off invasion in Scotland or Ireland. England was transformed into a much bigger kingdom, more secure from invasion, and ultimately more powerful because it was able to draw on a widening hinterland of resources, wealth and manpower at a time when that hinterland was itself expanding. This explains why England, less than six million people pitted against the twenty million Frenchmen, in 1689 could defy France in the long and increasingly expensive wars which dominated British history from 1689 to 1815. A result of this financial wealth was that England showed signs of becoming the war chest of France's enemies. If it did not have sufficient manpower to put in the field, it could sustain its European allies by subsidies or, as in the case of its campaigns in Ireland in 1690, by quite literally hiring 7000 troops from the king of Denmark. In the War of the Spanish Succession in the early eighteenth century, English money was even more vital than English manpower to England's allies.

Financial resources on this scale could only be tapped if they were readily available in a convenient centre. London, drawing on the wealth and business talent of all three kingdoms, played that role from the late seventeenth century onwards. It was already emerging in the seventeenth century as the largest city in Europe and by the end of the century it was also beginning to replace Amsterdam as the most important financial centre in Europe. Large colonies of Scots and Irishmen, who were contributing more and more to the management of Britain's growing trade, began to emerge in London.[10] Britain's huge tobacco trade by the 1740s was largely handled by the Scots, and its finances in those years when Scots replaced Englishmen in its conduct were ordered by two Irishmen in London, the two George Fitzgeralds, uncle and nephew respectively.[11] Britain's trade with Scandinavia, to the extent that it was not in the hands of expatriate Scandinavians, was conducted mainly by Scots, just as London's trade with Spain and France depended heavily on a network of Irish Catholic merchants in London and overseas.

Contrary to what people thought and still think, England was a much more centralised country than France. The greater of the English nobility were also individually much richer than their French counterparts.[12] A consequence was that, because they were politically powerful and spent much of their wealth in London, they drew to the capital a large portion of the wealth of the countryside. In France, by contrast, the typical nobleman was much more likely to spend his time and income in the provinces. A much smaller part of the wealth of the kingdom found its way to Paris. The fact that wealth was spent in the provinces, and that country gentry flocked to provincial cities for their amusement, made the provincial cities larger and more opulent than their English counterparts. Norwich, Newcastle, Liverpool or Bristol paled beside Bordeaux, Nantes, Rennes or Toulouse. On the other hand, London by the late eighteenth century was almost twice as large as Paris, and accounted for 12 per cent of the population of England and Wales while Paris counted for less than 3 per cent of French population. Versailles, the court city on the doorstep of Paris, might give the reverse impression simply because France was much the larger country and the aggregate expenditure of its courtiers outweighed the expenditure of the English court.

The English nobility, either with surplus cash in hand, or else seeking money to finance their social activities, developed close ties with the London financiers. Indeed, much of the political distinction between Whig and Tory lay in the clash between the country gentry who felt that wealth and social values should centre on the countryside and the Whig grandees whose alliance with financial interests gave them a cosmopolitan outlook and a leverage in court and parliament which made it possible for their views to prevail in foreign policy. In France no such broad amalgam of landed and financial interests developed. As a result, in wartime the smaller country, by borrowing from this rich circle, was able to match, pound for pound, the military expenditure of its much bigger and richer neighbour. Even in social terms, France, despite all its wealth, could not rival the dazzling concentration of all that was rich and handsome found in Bath.[13] Bath, a provincial town which was insignificant at the outset of the eighteenth century, contained seasonally a larger population than Versailles. The social ascendancy of Bath in the English social season was a peculiar and illuminating comment on the unity and cohesiveness of English upper-class life.

If England, the richest region in the British Isles, relied on the poorer periphery, Scotland and Ireland, for some of the capital necessary to finance the tasks of government, this was even truer of that other vital sinew of empire and war alike: manpower. This resource was, of course, more abundant than capital in the periphery. Even in the seventeenth century, this dependence was foreshadowed in the manner in which English colonisation came to depend on the manpower of the two sister kingdoms. After the early decades of the century, when disenchanted Englishmen had gone to Virginia and New England, rather few Englishmen crossed the Atlantic, and Scots and Irishmen were increasingly evident in the colonisation of both the West Indies and the mainland. Something of a demographic crisis in English population from the 1630s to the 1680s added to the swiftness of the transition.[14]

Most striking of all, Irishmen and Scots began to appear in the British army, and were gradually to become its backbone. The policy began at the Restoration when the Stuarts, manacled by parliament in England, built up an army of around 7000 men in Ireland. This policy was made still more systematic under William III and his successors, and the size of the army in Ireland was doubled to 12,000 men.[15] The huge military barracks of Ireland began to appear: the Royal Barracks in Dublin were reputedly the largest in Europe. The reason for this huge army was certainly not security in Ireland, for in wartime most of the army was whisked out of the country. The difference with Stuart policy was that the Williamite regiments were formed in England and then transferred to Irish stations in order to appear on the Irish payroll. The result was that one-half of the peacetime strength of the eighteenth-century army was carried by the Irish taxpayer.[16]

What was happening in Ireland began later in Scotland. The defeat of the invasion of Scotland in 1746 secured the London government from its last internal threat. Highlanders now began to move to the new world[17] and within the army the highlands were to become the most compact area of recruitment within the British Isles. In the Seven Years' War, faced with novel demands for military manpower, recruitment within Ireland and Scotland began to become more systematic; henceforth, about half the British army, rank and file, and a higher proportion of the officers, were to consist of Irishmen and Scots.[18] In other words, the periphery was increasingly vital for the maintenance of an army. In large part it both financed and now, as well, manned it.

Thus, by 1763, Scotland and Ireland carried much of the burden of peopling the colonies and, increasingly, the thankless lot of the common soldier. The inhabitants of England itself, richer, and with more worthwhile opportunities at home, less readily took to these tasks, in a sense reflecting the attitudes of the local gentry who were less enamoured of the outside world than the Whig magnates in London. The achievement of the elder Pitt as prime minister during the Seven Years' War was that his foreign policies were so successful that they allayed this deep distrust. For the first time, the distinction between Whig and Tory became meaningless.

If London prospered at the head of the resources and talents of these islands, Dublin and Edinburgh did so too as the channel of communications between their own hinterlands and London. Indeed, the success of this communion of interests within the British Isles centred on four cities: London, Bath, Dublin and Edinburgh, almost to the exclusion of other cities. In addition, Dublin was easily the largest city after London. Moreover, it was in the process of becoming

12.5. The Fourth Duke
of Atholl and his family

a planned city from the 1760s, and Edinburgh was to follow suit from the 1770s. Together with Bath, they were to become and remain the model of eighteenth-century urban elegance and planning. The planning of Edinburgh was still in the future, but Dublin's Wide Street Commissioners, established in 1757, had already set to work. Dublin's great aristocratic town houses were on a vast scale; there was never to be anything like them in Edinburgh, and they represented a prodigious effort by the Irish gentry and peerage to emulate their English counterparts. Dublin as a city was even remodelled on the pattern of London. Its second great square, and the elongated line of Gardiner's Mall were shaped in the 1750s, and the line of Merrion Square followed in the 1760s.

The drawing-in of Scottish and Irish manpower and capital into the pursuit of empire and war, and an increasingly London-orientated periphery, had a third and perhaps even more important concomitant, a greater common cultural heritage. If the periphery was exploited in manpower and resources for the benefit of metropolitan interests to a degree unrivalled in the eighteenth century elsewhere in Europe, the same was true in cultural terms. While a British culture emerged, the place of the periphery in British society meant that artists and writers from there were less at a disadvantage than in metropolitan cultures of other societies. If we confine ourselves to literature, for instance, it is immediately obvious that Scots and Irish were already carving a place for themselves in English letters altogether out of proportion to their numbers.

One aspect of the homogenisation of the British Isles that should not be overlooked is how British culture gained from the interaction of Scots in Ireland and at home. Scotland, though having only half the population of Ireland in the seventeenth century, was a very vigorous society, more unified than Ireland, not only politically but also culturally. It boasted four universities compared to Ireland's one and England's two. The influx of Scots to Ireland, part of the manifold vigour of Scotland, was large, and it created a forceful, well-knit local society, distrusted both by the Anglo-Irish landlords under whom they held land, and by the government in Dublin. A small pan-Scottish world grew up, characterised by constant coming and going across the narrow channel dividing Ireland and Scotland. Ulster Scots were educated in Scotland, especially in Glasgow University which, in turn, was to draw the intellectual vigour that made it the shining light of the Scottish enlightenment from the width of its catchment area.

The influx of the Scots in the north and of English settlers widely, but thinly, elsewhere created for the first time an effective, English-speaking society in Ireland. It was a new world narrowing the wide gap which had hitherto separated Ireland in language and culture from England. Anglo-Irish landlords dominated Irish society at the top, even when their tenants were Presbyterian Scots. By 1700 a quarter of the population, compared with a mere 1 or 2 per cent in 1600, were of Scottish or English origin. The first housing in the villages was distinctly English in style, contrasting with the indigenous houses, or with the houses of the Scots at home or in Ireland. The villages, too, represented a paternalistic and hierarchical social order, standing at the gates of the castle or house of their founder or protector.

The cultural character of Scotland and Ireland was all the more different because Scotland experienced no influx of settlers, whereas Ireland was massively settled from Britain and the indigenous landed class rooted out. The Scots looked to their own universities, church and law courts. On the other hand, the established church in Ireland was Anglican, and the law was based on English law. Unlike Scots, gentry sons, if they received a higher education, typically completed it by finishing at the Inns of Court in London. The Irish gentry, too, not only because of their origins but because individually they were larger and grander than their Scottish counterparts, kept up their English contacts. Dublin flowered in the middle of the eighteenth century as the largest provincial exposition of London culture,[19] and in turn,

Irish literary figures found it easy to make their careers in London, whereas many, although not all, Scots made their name at home. Put crudely, there were more and richer Irishmen than Scots to be found in the season at Bath. As a consequence of these differences, the cultural responses of Scotland and Ireland in the age of enlightenment were different.

Scotland, because of its independent and, indeed, parochial institutions developed speculative thought in a remarkable way. Francis Hutcheson, an Ulster-Scot at Glasgow University, was the father of this, but the greatest names in its intellectual flowering were to be David Hume and Adam Smith. The accents of literature were often local too, and Robert Burns' poetry was hailed despite its expression in lowland Scots. The tartan plaid and the kilt became a sentimental rage. Scots gentry, too, danced Scottish dances as well as the dances fashionable at the London court. In Ireland, by contrast, local accents were studiously avoided in literature, and traditional dances and dress were spurned by the gentry. Paradoxically, the presence of a parliament of its own, in contrast to Edinburgh, which had lost its assembly in 1707, did not support independence in culture in Ireland but simply provided patronage for the high culture of Anglican and gentry England.

In Ireland, the church and laws were modelled on English precedents, the judiciary and episcopal sees were largely filled with Englishmen, and Irishmen were studiously avoided in the eighteenth century as the king's representatives in Ireland. This fact revealed the deep distrust by English politicians of their Irish Protestant colony, and the wide gulf which separated London from Dublin. As broader imperial views emerged in London in the 1750s and 1760s, the gulf became wider. The empire, too, was peopled more by Irish Presbyterians and Catholics than by Irish Anglicans.

An Irishman of Catholic background, Edmund Burke, establishing himself in English public life at the outset of the 1760s, was to be the greatest spokesman of Britain's imperial role. As a provincial, he was appreciative of the opportunities the empire afforded to the periphery, and for the same reason he was sympathetic to the rights of the colonists within the empire. Burke, however, even if politically the most articulate of the Irishmen and Scots who descended upon London, was only one of many. Samuel Johnson, that most English of Englishmen, had an Englishman's view of this when he expostulated that the noblest prospect facing a Scotsman was the road to London.[20] An Irishman had indeed noted in 1760 that 'an imagination that London is a kind of paradise and that England in general is very much like it, is the occasion of such numbers of my countrymen as swarm in London in all occupations'.[21]

Further reading

L.M. Cullen, *The Emergence of Modern Ireland 1600–1900*, 2nd edn (Dublin, 1983); F.G. James, *Ireland in the Empire, 1688–1770* (Cambridge, Mass., 1973); B. Lenman, *Integration, Enlightenment and Industrialisation: Scotland 1746–1832* (London, 1981); P.W.J. Riley, *The Union of England and Scotland* (Manchester, 1978); D.B. Quinn and A.N. Ryan, *England's Sea Empire 1550–1642* (London, 1983); T.C. Smout, *A History of the Scottish People, 1560–1830* (London, 1969); B. Williams, *The Whig Supremacy, 1714–1760* (Oxford, 1962).

Notes

1. The Reformation *Christopher Haigh*

1. Foxe's influence is discussed in W. Haller, *Foxe's Book of Martyrs and the Elect Nation* (London, 1963), and can still be detected in A.G. Dickens, *The English Reformation* (London, 1964) which is the best modern study of our subject.
2. See C. Haigh, 'The Recent Historiography of the English Reformation', *Historical Journal* 25 (1982).
3. The approach of this essay is much influenced by the work of D.R. Starkey, conveniently summarised in his 'From Feud to Faction', *History Today* (1982).
4. See P. Williams, *The Tudor Regime* (Oxford, 1979).
5. For different versions of the uncertain politics of Henry's last years, see Starkey, 'From Feud to Faction', and L.B. Smith, 'Henry VIII and the Protestant Triumph', *American Historical Review* 71 (1966).
6. A new study of Mary's accession is urgently needed. There is useful material in D. MacCulloch (ed.), 'Vita Mariae', *Camden Miscellany* 28 (1984).
7. The making of the 'settlement' is discussed in N.L. Jones, *Faith by Statute* (Royal Historical Society Studies in History, 1982).
8. W.T. MacCaffrey, *The Shaping of the Elizabethan Regime* (Princeton, 1968), pp. 103–5; W.T. MacCaffrey, *Queen Elizabeth and the Making of Policy, 1572–1588* (Princeton, 1981), ch. 11.
9. P. Hughes (ed.), *St. John Fisher: the Earliest English Life* (London, 1935), p. 160.
10. Jones, *Faith by Statute*, p. 150.
11. C. Haigh, 'The Church of England, the Catholics and the People', in *The Reign of Elizabeth I* (Basingstoke, 1984), pp. 195–9.
12. The attraction of Protestantism is best conveyed by A.G. Dickens, *The English Reformation*, and P. Collinson, *The Religion of Protestants* (Oxford, 1982). Literacy rates are calculated in D. Cressy, *Literacy and the Social Order* (Cambridge, 1980).
13. The process can be traced through R. Hutton, 'The Local Impact of the Tudor Reformations', in C. Haigh (ed.), *The English Reformation Revised* (Cambridge, 1986); and the response of parishioners observed

in J.J. Scarisbrick, *The Reformation and the English People* (Oxford, 1984), chs 5–6.

14. There is a good, brief survey of the Reformation in Scotland in J. Wormald, *Court, Kirk and Community: Scotland 1470–1625* (London, 1981), chs 5–8. The classic modern study is G. Donaldson, *The Scottish Reformation* (Cambridge, 1960).

15. P. Collinson, 'The Elizabethan Church and the New Religion', in Haigh (ed.), *The Reign of Elizabeth I*, ch. 7.

16. W. Hinde, *A Faithful Remonstrance of the Holy Life and Happy Death of John Bruen* (London, 1641), pp. 210–12.

17. Ibid., pp. 83–4.

18. Haigh, 'The Church of England, the Catholics and the People', pp. 205–16; K. Wrightson, *English Society, 1580–1680* (London, 1982), ch. 7; P. Clark, *The English Alehouse* (Harlow, 1983), ch. 7.

19. C. Haigh, 'From Monopoly to Minority: Catholicism in Early Modern England', *Transactions of the Royal Historical Society*, 5th series 31 (1981).

20. K. Thomas, *Religion and the Decline of Magic* (London, 1971).

21. M. Spufford, *Small Books and Pleasant Histories* (London, 1981), p. 34.

22. W.J. Sheils, *The Puritans in the Diocese of Peterborough* (Northants Record Society, 1979), pp. 37, 68–9, 131.

23. Cheshire County Record Office, EDV1/14, fos 186–7.

2.   The Governance of Tudor England   *David Starkey*

1. Sir Thomas Smith, *De Republica Anglorum* (London, 1583), p. 47.

2. British Library, Harley MS 1419 A, fos 115, 151.

3. The most useful discussion of Tudor government is Penry Williams, *The Tudor Regime* (Oxford, 1979).

4. The best description of Tudor Westminster is *The History of the King's Works*, ed. H.M. Colvin *et al.*, IV, ii (London, 1982), pp. 286ff.; while payments for the 1527 reception are in the Public Record Office, E 36/227, fo. 3 v.

5. J.D. Alsop, 'Government, Finance and the Community of the Exchequer' in *The Reign of Elizabeth I*, ed. Christopher Haigh (London, 1984), pp. 102–3.

6. For Henry VIII's palaces see Colvin, *King's Works*.

7. For the continuing activity of king and household in government see *Revolution Reassessed*, ed. C.H.D. Coleman and David Starkey (Oxford, 1986).

8. This approach is developed more fully in David Starkey, 'The Age of the Household', in *The Later Middle Ages*, ed. Stephen Medcalf (London, 1981).

9. J.B. Trapp and H.S. Herbruggen, *'The King's Good Servant': Sir Thomas More, 1477/8–1535* (London, 1977), p. 31.

10. Elias Ashmole, *The Institution, Laws and Ceremonies of the Most Noble Order of the Garter* (London, 1672), appendix; Richard Marks and Ann Payne, *British Heraldry* (London, 1978), pp. 237ff.

11. David Starkey, 'Ightham Mote: Politics and Architecture in Early Tudor England', *Archaeologia*, 107 (1981).

12. *Letters and Papers of the Reign of Henry VIII* ('L.P.'), ed. J.S. Brewer *et al.*, IV, ii, no. 4188 (London, 1862–1932).

13. *L.P.*, V, nos. 1051, 1130: VI, no. 547.

14. *Ingulph's Chronicle of the Abbey of Croyland*, trans. H.T. Riley (London, 1854), pp. 480, 483–4.

15. Sir John Fortescue, *The Governance of England*, ed. Charles Plummer (Oxford, 1885), pp. 150–1.

16. British Library, Cotton MS. Titus B i, fo. 192.

17. David Cressy, 'Binding the Nation', in *Tudor Rule and Revolution*, ed. D.J. Guth and J.W. McKenna (Cambridge, 1982).

18. Edward Hall, *The Union of the Two Noble and Illustre Families of Lancaster and York* (London, 1809), p. 599.

19. Penry Williams in *The Tudor Regime* has some very good things to say on royal servants and retaining, pp. 109ff.

20. The argument for a 'Tudor revolution in government' is G.R. Elton's and is presented most recently in his *Reform and Reformation* (London, 1977).

21. The best recent sketch of Elizabethan government and politics is Simon Adams, 'Eliza Enthrone' in Haigh, *The Reign of Elizabeth I*.

22. *The Works of Edmund Spenser*, ed. R. Morris (London, 1904), p. 521.

23. The problem is discussed in Joel Hurstfield, 'Political Corruption in Modern England', *History*, 52 (1967).

3.   The First King of Britain   *Jenny Wormald*

1. W.C. Sellars and R.J. Yeatman, *1066 and All That* (London, 1975 reprint), p. 69.

2. The underlying theme of S.R. Gardiner's magisterial *History of England from the Accession of James I to the Outbreak of the Civil War* (10 vols, 1883–4), a work of most impressive scholarship. Also, for example, W. Notestein, *The Winning of the Initiative by the House of Commons* (Raleigh Lecture, 1924) and *The House of Commons, 1604–1610* (New Haven, 1971).

3. N. Davies, *God's Playground: A History of Poland* (Oxford, 1981), I, pp. 413–20, 433–7; J.H. Elliott, *Europe Divided, 1559–1598* (London, 1968), pp. 276–81; G. Parker, *Europe in Crisis, 1598–1648* (Glasgow, 1979), pp. 257–63. James's speech to parliament is in *The Political Works of James I*, ed. C.H. McIlwain (New York, reprint 1965), pp. 290–305.

4. The Perfect Description is in P. Hume Brown, *Early Travellers In Scotland* (Edinburgh, reprint 1978), pp. 96–103; *The Court and*

Character is in *The Secret History of the Court of James ı*, ed. Walter Scott (Edinburgh, 1811), I, pp. 1–298, II, pp. 1–20.

5. J.M. Brown (now Wormald), 'Scottish Politics, 1567–1625', in *The Reign of James vı and ı*, ed. A.G.R. Smith (London, 1973), pp. 22–39; J. Wormald, *Court, Kirk and Community: Scotland 1470–1625* (London, 1981), ch. 1.

6. G. Donaldson, 'The Scottish Church, 1567–1625' in *James vı and ı*, ed. Smith, pp. 40–56; Donaldson, *Scotland: James v–vıı* (Edinburgh, 1965), ch. 11.

7. G.G. Simpson, *Scottish Handwriting 1150–1650* (Edinburgh, 1973), pp. 8–12; M. Lee Jr, *John Maitland of Thirlestane* (Princeton, 1959); K.M. Brown, *The Scottish Bloodfeud, 1573–1625: Politics, Violence and Justice in an Early Modern Society* (Edinburgh, 1986), ch. 6; Wormald, *Court, Kirk and Community*, chs 9, 10.

8. The case for Buckingham as a major political figure has been convincingly argued by R. Lockyer, *Buckingham* (London, 1981).

9. *Political Works*, ed. McIlwain, pp. 3–70; *The Basilikon Doron of King James vı*, ed. J. Craigie (Scottish Text Society, Edinburgh, 1944–50).

10. Bodleian Library, Oxford, Ashmole MS. 1729, ff. 39r–90v; Public Record Office, SP 14/2/96.

11. Margaret MacCurtain, *Tudor and Stuart Ireland* (Gill History of Ireland 7, Dublin, 1972), chs 5, 6; M. Percival-Maxwell, *The Scottish Migration to Ulster in the Reign of James ı* (London, 1973).

12. PRO SP 14/7/59; D.H. Willson, 'Relations between Scotland and England in the Early Seventeenth Century', in *Proceedings of the First Colloquium on Scottish Studies*, I (University of Guelph, 1968), pp. 1–25. The most detailed and balanced analysis of the issue of union is in B.R. Galloway, 'The Union of England and Scotland, 1603–1608' (Cambridge PhD thesis, 1982).

13. Ashmole MS. 1729, ff. 39r, 51r, 56r–v.

14. K. Sharpe, 'Parliamentary History 1603–1629: In or out of Perspective', in *Faction and Parliament: Essays on Early Stuart History*, ed. Sharpe (Oxford, 1978), pp. 1–42; R.C. Munden, 'James ı and "the growth of mutual distrust": King, Commons and Reform, 1603–1604', ibid. pp. 43–72. Linda Levy Peck, *Northampton: Patronage and Policy at the Court of James ı* (London, 1982) and her articles there cited. C. Russell, *Parliaments and English Politics, 1621–29* (Oxford, 1979), esp. ch. 1; J. Wormald, 'James vı and ı: Two Kings or One?', *History* 68 (1983), pp. 199–209. S.L. Adams, 'Foreign Policy and the Parliaments of 1621 and 1624', in *Faction and Parliament*, ed. Sharpe, pp. 139–71, and Adams, 'Spain or the Netherlands? The Dilemma of Early Stuart Foreign Policy' in *Before the English Civil War*, ed. H. Tomlinson (London, 1983), pp. 79–101. N. Tyacke, 'Puritanism, Arminianism and Counter-Revolution', in *The Origins of the English Civil War*, ed. C. Russell (London, 1973), pp. 119–43; P. Collinson, *The Religion of Protestants* (Oxford, 1982); P. Lake and K. Fincham, The Ecclesiastical Policy of James ı', *Journal of British Studies* 24 (1985), pp. 169–207.

15. Edward Nicholas, *Proceedings and Debates of the House of Commons in 1620 and 1621* (Oxford, 1766), I, pp. 2–3; R. Zaller, *The Parliament of 1621* (Berkeley, 1971), pp. 31–2.
16. British Library, Additional MS. 4160, ff. 265r–6v. For Dunbar's career, see M. Lee Jr, *Government by Pen* (Urbana, 1980), especially ch. 3.
17. *The Poetical Works of Alexander Craig of Rosecraig*, ed. D. Laing (Hunterian Club 2, Glasgow, 1873), p. 1.

4.   Crown and Parliament   *Kevin Sharpe*

1. See, for example, Bates's case in G.W. Prothero (ed.), *Selected Statutes and Other Constitutional Documents* (Oxford, 1964), p. 40 and the speech of Justice Berkeley in Hampden's case in S.R. Gardiner (ed.), *The Constitutional Documents of the Puritan Revolution* (Oxford, 1899), pp. 115–23.
2. R.W.K. Hinton, 'English Constitutional Theories from Sir John Fortescue to Sir John Eliot', *English Historical Review* 85 (1960), pp. 410–25.
3. See the speech of Sir Thomas Wentworth in J.P. Kenyon (ed.), *The Stuart Constitution* (Cambridge, 1966), pp. 18–19.
4. W.H. Greenleaf, *Order, Empiricism and Politics: Two Traditions of English Political Thought* (London, 1964); R. Eccleshall, *Order and Reason in Politics* (Oxford, 1978).
5. L. Boynton, *The Elizabethan Militia, 1558–1638* (London, 1967).
6. G.E. Aylmer, *The King's Servants. The Civil Service of Charles I* (London, 1961).
7. C. Russell, 'Parliamentary History in Perspective, 1604–29', *History* 61 (1976), pp. 1–27; D. Thomas, 'Financial and Administrative Developments', in H. Tomlinson (ed.), *Before the English Civil War* (London, 1983), pp. 103–22.
8. J. Wormald, 'James VI and I: Two Kings or One?', *History* 68 (1983), pp. 187–209.
9. R. Strong, *Charles I on Horseback* (London, 1972); S. Orgel, *The Illusion of Power* (Berkeley, 1975); S. Orgel and R. Strong, *Inigo Jones: The Theatre of the Stuart Court*, 2 vols (London, 1973).
10. As Bishop John Williams observed. See J. Hacket, *Scrinia Reserata. A Memorial offered to the great deserving of John Williams* (two parts, 1693), II, p. 8.
11. C. Russell, *Parliaments and English Politics, 1621–29* (Oxford, 1979).
12. K. Sharpe, 'The Personal Rule of Charles I', in Tomlinson (ed.), *Before the English Civil War*, pp. 52–78.
13. For good studies of local government and local responses see A. Fletcher, *A County Community in Peace and War. Sussex 1600–1660* (London, 1975); T.G. Barnes, *Somerset, 1625–42* (London, 1961); J.S. Morrill, *Cheshire, 1630–1660* (Oxford, 1974) and *The Revolt of the Provinces* (London, 1976).

14. D. Stevenson, *The Scottish Revolution 1637–1644* (Newton Abbott, 1973).

15. K. Sharpe, 'Crown, Parliament and Locality: Government and Communication in early modern England', *English Historical Review* (forthcoming).

16. Sharpe, 'The Personal Rule of Charles ɪ'.

17. Morrill, *Revolt of the Provinces.*

18. C. Hibbard, *Charles ɪ and The Popish Plot* (Chapel Hill, 1983).

19. E. Cope, *Proceedings of the Short Parliament* (Camden Society, 1977).

20. C. Russell, 'The Nature of a Parliament in Early Stuart England', in Tomlinson (ed.), *Before the English Civil War*, pp. 141–50.

21. The best account of the period 1640 to 1642 is A. Fletcher, *The Outbreak of the English Civil War* (London, 1981).

5. 'For King and Country' *Ronald Hutton*

1. Richard Gough, *Human Nature Displayed in the History of Myddle* (London, 1834), p. 31.

2. From the original, preserved by John Prideaux-Brune, Esq., at Prideaux Place, Padstow.

3. Letter X in Thomas Carlyle (ed.), *Letter and Speeches of Oliver Cromwell* (edition by S.C. Lomas, 1904).

4. Letter XXI in the same edition.

5. Letter CIV in the same edition.

6. J.W. Willis-Bund (ed.), *The Diary of Henry Townshend* (Worcestershire Historical Society, 1915–20), vol. II, pp. 238–9.

7. Printed in *Perfect Occurances* (21 November 1645).

8. In Shropshire Record Office, Box 298.

9. Isaac Tullie, *A Narrative of the Siege of Carlisle* (1840), n.p.

10. Kent Archives Office, Sackville Correspondence.

11. Bodleian Library, Firth MS. C7, f. 251.

12. Bodleian Library, Tanner MS. 60, f. 206.

13. Kent Archives Office, De La Warre MSS, Berkshire to Bath 6 June 1645.

6. Restoration and the Rise of Party *Mark Goldie*

1. Sir Edward Turner, May 1661: *The Parliamentary History of England* (London, 1808), vol. IV, col. 202. He went on to observe that 'as the former spirit of reformation at first brought us into this misery; so the spirit of giddiness, which God sent amongst our reformers, at length cured us'.

2. The standard account is J.H. Plumb, *The Growth of Political Stability in England 1675–1725* (London, 1967). Recently Geoffrey Holmes has provided a magisterial survey of the bases of the gentry's success: 'The Achievement of Stability: the Social Context of Politics from the 1680s

to the Age of Walpole', in J. Cannon (ed.), *The Whig Ascendancy* (London, 1981).

3. Samuel Butler, *Hudibras*, ed. J. Wilders (Oxford, 1967), p. 7.

4. See J. Cannon, *Parliamentary Reform 1640–1832* (Cambridge, 1973).

5. See R.S. Bosher, *The Making of the Restoration Settlement* (London, 1951); I.M. Green, *The Re-establishment of the Church of England 1660–1663* (Oxford, 1978); J.H. Pruett, *The Parish Clergy under the Later Stuarts: The Leicestershire Experience* (Urbana, Illinois, 1978). (The prayer book formularies of the 1662 Act of Uniformity remained standard until the 1970s, and many Anglican churchgoers still regret the passing of '1662'.)

6. For a brilliant case-study of the politics and attitudes of the county gentry elite see P. Jenkins, *The Making of a Ruling Class: The Glamorgan Gentry 1640–1790* (Cambridge, 1983).

7. Parliament has sat every year since 1689, and therefore only from that date did it truly become a permanent part of government. The Triennial Act was renewed in 1694 and since then regular general elections have been statutorily required, although the term was modified to seven years in 1716, and to our present five years in 1910.

8. See J.R. Western, *Monarchy and Revolution: The English State in the 1680s* (London, 1972); J.R. Jones (ed.), *The Restored Monarchy 1660–1688* (London, 1979).

9. Traditionally, the first prime minister is said to be Sir Robert Walpole (1721–42), but both Danby (1673–9) and Sir Robert Harley (1710–14) have good claims. The term 'premier minister' was occasionally used throughout the Restoration period.

10. Most historians of the Restoration are agreed on these claims. But historians of the Civil War insist that the events of mid-century were a true revolutionary transformation of English politics and society. It is worth remembering that our Hanoverian and Victorian forebears took for granted that *the* Revolution was that of 1688–9, and only in the past half-century has the phrase 'the English Revolution' been transferred to the 1640s. For a valuable reopening of this question see A. McInnes, 'When was the English Revolution?', *History* 67 (1982), pp. 377–92.

11. The first oath, the 'non-resistance' oath, was included in the Militia, Uniformity and Corporation Acts of 1661–2. The second, the 'no alteration' oath, was proposed by Danby in 1675, but defeated by his opponents, led by the earl of Shaftesbury.

12. See J.P. Kenyon, *The Popish Plot* (London, 1974); J. Miller, *Popery and Politics in England 1660–1688* (Cambridge, 1973). The murdered magistrate was Sir Edmund Berry Godfrey; James's executed secretary was Fr Edward Coleman. The last victim of Plot fever was the Irish archbishop Oliver Plunkett, executed in 1681; in 1981 Catholics held a tercentennial commemorative Mass on Clapham Common.

13. See K.H.D. Haley, *The First Earl of Shaftesbury* (Oxford, 1968). Good modern political biographies of Restoration figures are thin on the

ground; one other which stands out is J.P. Kenyon, *Robert Spencer, Earl of Sunderland* (London, 1958).

14. The Tory Sir Jonathan Trelawny versus the Whig William Ash, November 1678: *Parliamentary History*, vol. IV, col. 1045.

15. See P. Earle, *Monmouth's Rebels* (London, 1977).

16. These Declarations, and all the major contemporary political documents, are printed in J.P. Kenyon (ed.), *The Stuart Constitution 1603–1688: Documents and Commentary* (Cambridge, 1966).

17. On the Revolution and its aftermath see J.R. Jones, *The Revolution of 1688 in England* (London, 1972); J. Carswell, *The Descent on England* (New York, 1969); J. Miller, *The Glorious Revolution* (London, 1983); G. Holmes (ed.), *Britain after the Glorious Revolution 1689–1714* (London, 1969). (The Act of Settlement is still sometimes a live issue, arousing the religious feelings of the seventeenth century, such as in the case of the row over the Prince of Wales' visit to the Vatican in April 1985; the Act, as *The Times* stated, forbids those who may inherit the crown to 'hold communion with the See or Church of Rome'.)

18. The themes explored in this chapter will receive extended treatment in M. Goldie, *The Tory Ideology: Politics, Religion, and Ideas in Restoration England* (Cambridge, forthcoming).

7. Revolution to Robinocracy   *William Speck*

1. For the contrary view that most Tories were committed to a Stuart restoration under the first two Georges, see Eveline Cruickshanks, *Political Untouchables: the Tories and the Forty-five* (1979).

2. See G.V. Bennett, *The Tory Crisis in Church and State 1688–1730* (1975).

3. See Geoffrey Holmes, *The Trial of Dr Sacheverell* (1973).

4. See P.G.M. Dickson, *The Financial Revolution* (1967).

5. J.H. Plumb, *The Growth of Political Stability in England 1675–1725* (London, 1967), p. 172.

6. Cf. Linda Colley, 'Eighteenth-century English radicalism before Wilkes', *Transactions of the Royal Historical Society* 31 (1981), pp. 1–20.

7. N. Rogers, 'Riot and Popular Jacobitism in Early Hanoverian England', in *Ideology and Conspiracy: Aspects of Jacobitism 1689–1759*, ed. Eveline Cruickshanks (Edinburgh, 1982), pp. 70–88.

8. E.P. Thompson, *Whigs and Hunters* (1975).

9. Geoffrey Holmes, 'The Achievement of Stability: the Social Context of Politics from the 1680s to the Age of Walpole', in *The Whig Ascendancy: Colloquies on Hanoverian England*, ed. J. Cannon (1981), pp. 1–22.

10. E.A. Wrigley and R.S. Schofield, *The Population History of England 1541–1871* (1981), pp. 207–11.

11. Geoffrey Holmes, *Augustan England: Professions, State and Society 1680–1730* (1982).

8. Love, Marriage and Death *Keith Wrightson*

Notes have been confined to identifying the sources of quotations.

1. The quotations are drawn from two contemporary descriptions of English society, those of William Harrison and Guy Miege. See F.J. Furnivall (ed.), *Harrison's Description of England*, New Shakespeare Society, 6th series, No. 1 (London, 1877), p. 134; D.A. Baugh (ed.), *Aristocratic Government and Society in Eighteenth-Century England* (New York, 1975), p. 47.
2. Essex Record Office Q/5 Ba 2/7; University of Durham Department of Palaeography and Diplomatic DRV II; M.J. Ingram, 'Ecclesiastical Justice in Wiltshire 1600–1640 (Oxford University D.Phil thesis, 1976), p. 106.
3. A fuller account of Henry Abbot's life, together with an admirable introduction to the records which can be used to reconstruct village life in this period, can be found in Alan Macfarlane (in collaboration with Sarah Harrison and Charles Jardine), *Reconstructing Historical Communities* (Cambridge, 1977). For Henry Abbot see pp. 70–2 and 140–50.
4. W.G. Hoskins, 'Harvest fluctuations and English economic history, 1480–1619', *Agricultural History Review* 12 (1964), p. 40.
5. The contemporary was James I's attorney general, quoted in C. Holmes, *Seventeenth-Century Lincolnshire* (Lincoln, 1980), p. 29.
6. Quoted in D.M. Stenton, *The English Woman in History* (London, 1957), p. 105.
7. T.F. Merrill (ed.), *William Perkins, 1558–1602 English Puritanist: His Pioneer Works on Casuistry* (The Hague, 1966), pp. 427–8.
8. R. Parkinson (ed.), *The Life of Adam Martindale, Written by Himself*, Chetham Society, Old Series, vol. 4 (1845), p. 16.
9. W.L. Sachse (ed.), *The Diary of Roger Lowe, 1663–74* (London, 1938), pp. 21, 68, 119.
10. M. Spufford, *Small Books and Pleasant Histories* (London, 1981), p. 60.
11. See note 7 above.
12. University of Durham Department of Palaeography and Diplomatic, Probate, Will of Edward Newby (1659).
13. E. Hughes, *North Country Life in the Eighteenth Century. The North-East, 1700–1750* (Oxford, 1952), p. 37.
14. L.A. Pollock, *Forgotten Children* (Cambridge, 1983), p. 135.
15. Parkinson (ed.), *Life of Adam Martindale*, p. 154.

9. Buying and Selling *Margaret Spufford*

Dr Spufford would like to thank Mr Dennis Jeeps of Willingham, Dr Victor Morgan of the University of East Anglia, Mrs Dorothy Owen of the University of Cambridge, and The Pepys Librarian, Magdalene College, Cambridge for help with material.

1. William Harrison, *Description of England* (first edn 1577), ed. G. Edelen (New York, 1968), pp. 200–1.
2. Richard Carew, *Survey of Cornwall* (1723 edn), p. 66b.
3. *Deserted Medieval Villages*, ed. M. Beresford and J.G. Hurst (1971), ch. 2, p. 122.
4. 'Robert Loder's Farm Accounts, 1610–20', ed. G.E. Fussell, Camden Third Series LIII (1936).
5. For example, Nicholas Hill, baker, 1590 in 'Household and Farm Inventories in Oxfordshire, 1550–90' ed. M.A. Havinden, *Ox. Rec. Soc.* (1965), pp. 303–4.
6. *Housing*. W.G. Hoskins, 'The Rebuilding of Rural England, 1570–1640', first published 1953, reprinted in his *Provincial England* (London, 1965), pp. 131–48. Criticised by R. Machin, 'The Great Rebuilding: a Reassessment', *Past and Present* 77 (1977), pp. 33–56.
7. For population, see E.A. Wrigley and R.S. Schofield, *The Population History of England, 1541–1871: A Reconstruction* (London, 1981). Brief summary in R.M. Smith, 'Population and its Geography in England, 1500–1730', in *An Historical Geography of England and Wales*, ed. R.A. Dodgshon and R.A. Butlin (1978), pp. 199–237.
8. In case this should be taken as an example of the 'Protestant work ethic', the devout Catholic merchant of Prato was doing exactly the same thing round 1400.
9. *The Agrarian History of England and Wales*, IV, *1500–1640*, ed. Joan Thirsk (Cambridge, 1967) and V, *1640–1750* (Cambridge, 1985). Especially vol. IV, chs 3, on farming techniques, 8, on marketing, 9, on agricultural prices, and vol. V, Statistical Appendices.
10. Carolina Lane, 'The Development of Pasture and Meadows during the Sixteenth and Seventeenth Centuries', *Ag. Hist. Rev.* 28 (1980), part I.
11. Michael Havinden, 'Progress in Open-Field Oxfordshire', *Ag. Hist. Rev.* 9 (1961), II, pp. 79–81.
12. Margaret Spufford, *The Great Reclothing of Rural England: Petty Chapmen and their Wares in the Seventeenth Century* (Hambledon, 1984), Introduction and pp. 115–18.
13. 'Rural Economy in Yorkshire in 1641, being the Farming and Account Books of Henry Best of Elmswell in the East Riding of the County of York', ed. C.B. Robinson, *Surtees Soc.* XXXIII (1857), pp. 161–2.
14. J.A. Chartres, 'The Capital's Provincial Eyes: London's Inns in the Early Eighteenth Century', *London Journal* 3, no. 1 (1977), pp. 24–39. For transport in general, John Chartres, *Internal Trade in England, 1500–1700* (London, 1977) and 'Road Carrying in England in the Seventeenth Century: Myth and Reality', *Econ. Hist. Rev.*, 2nd Series 30 (1977); Alan Everitt, 'The Marketing of Agricultural Produce', chapter 8 in Thirsk (ed.), *Agrarian History*, IV.
15. *The Trade of England Revived*, abstracted in *Seventeenth Century Economic Documents*, ed. Joan Thirsk and J.P. Cooper (Oxford, 1972), pp. 329–30.
16. There is a discussion of James Leach's shop, along with a group of

probate inventories listing the contents of small shops, and the new Kentish ready-made clothes shops in M. Spufford, *Great Reclothing*, pp. 66–7, 172–224. Pedlars' inventories are printed as pp. 151–71.

17. David Cressy, *Literacy and the Social Order: Reading and Writing in Tudor and Stuart England* (Cambridge, 1980), on counting signatures, and Margaret Spufford, *Small Books and Pleasant Histories* (Cambridge, 1985), ch. 2, on the spread of reading skills.

18. Margaret Spufford, *Contrasting Communities: English Villagers in the Sixteenth and Seventeenth Centuries* (Cambridge, 1979), chs 5, 7 and 13 for the economy of Willingham, literacy, and scribes there.

19. Bernard Capp, *Astrology and the Popular Press, English Almanacs, 1500–1800* (London, 1979).

10. Language and Literature: Caxton to the Royal Society *Elizabeth Cook*

1. Edmund Rive writes, 'it is impossible for an English person throughly to understand his own language. to speake or write it rightly, without the skill of Latine'. *An Heptaglottologie* (London, 1618), p. 27, quoted by R.F. Jones, *The Triumph of the English Language* (Stanford, 1953), p. 277).

2. John Milton, *The Doctrine and Discipline of Divorce* (London, 1644), f. A4^v (this is the second 'revis'd and much augmented' edition; the first was 1643).

3. *An Exact Copy of the Last Will and Testament of Sir Thomas Cresham* (London, 1724), p. 38.

4. Virgil's *Aeneid* translated into Scottish English by Gavin Douglas was published 1553; George Chapman's translation of Homer's *Iliad* was published in 1610 and his *Odyssey* in 1616; Arthur Golding's translation of Ovid's *Metamorphoses* appeared in 1565; Philemon Holland's translation of Plutarch's *Roman Questions* appeared in 1603; Thomas Hobbes published his translation of Thucydides' *Eight Bookes of the Pelopennesian Warre* in 1629; Sir Thomas Hoby's translation of Castiglione's *The Book of the Courtier*, was published in 1561; John Florio's translation of Montaigne's *Essays* was published in 1603; the first part of Sir Thomas Urquhart's translation of Rabelais' *Gargantua* appeared in 1653.

5. For the history of the translation of the Bible into English see F.F. Bruce, *The English Bible* (London, 1970).

6. John Gerarde, *The Herball or Generall Historie of Plantes* (London, 1597), B 3^v.

7. Ibid., pp. 108–11.

8. From the dedication of the *Epitome* dated Padua, 13 August 1542; quoted and translated in Harvey Cushing, *A Bio-Bibliography of Andreas Vesalius (London, 1962), p. 111.

9. *The Oxford English Dictionary* gives an example from 1541 as the earliest use of *anatomy*.

10. Thomas Geminus, *Compendiosa totius Anatomiae delineatio* (London, 1559); the majority of the plates in this volume are copies of Calcar's extraordinary and beautiful illustrations to Vesalius' work.

11. This was followed up by Thomas Blount, *A World of Errors discovered in the New World of Words* (London, 1673).

12. Jones, *Triumph of the English Language*, op. cit., gives an excellent survey of the ideas about the English language being discussed at this time.

13. Thomas Elyot, *The boke named the Gouernour* (London, 1531), fol. 94v.

14. John Cheke, *Gospel According to St Matthew*, ed. James Goodwin (London, 1843).

15. *Ben Jonson*, ed. C.H. Herford, P. & E. Simpson (Oxford, 1954), vol. VIII, p. 618.

16. Philip Sidney, *A Defence of Poetry*, ed. J. Van Dorsten (Oxford, 1971), pp. 72–3.

17. William Salesbury, *A Dictionary in Englyshe and Welshe moche necessary to all suche Welshemen as wil spedly learne the englyshe tongue* (1547); *A playne and familiar Introduction, teaching how to pronounce the letters in the Brytishe tongue now commonly called Welshe* (1550). A second, enlarged, edition followed in 1567.

18. *The Anatomical Exercises of Dr William Harvey, De Motu Cordis, 1628, De Circulatione Sanguinis, 1649, The First English Text of 1653*, ed. Geoffrey Keynes (London, 1928), pp. 6, 49, 54.

19. *New Organum*, I. cxx in *The Works of Francis Bacon*, ed. James Spedding (London, 1857–74), vol. IV, pp. 106–7.

20. Sidney, *Defence of Poetry*, p. 72.

21. From the Preface 'The Translators to the Reader' which is printed in some (though few modern) editions of the King James Bible.

22. Thomas Hobbes, *Leviathan* (1651) ed. C.B. Macpherson (Harmondsworth, 1968), p. 106.

23. John Wilkins, *An Essay Towards a Real Character and a Philosophical Language* (London, 1668), p. 405.

24. Samuel Johnson, *A Dictionary of the English Language*, 2 vols (London, 1755), vol. I, fol. C.

11. Trade and Territory. The Rise of Imperial Britain 1603–1763   *Bruce Lenman*

1. Arthur H. Williamson, *Scottish National Consciousness in the Age of James VI* (Edinburgh, 1979).

2. Brendan Bradshaw, *The Irish Constitutional Revolution of the Sixteenth Century* (Cambridge, 1979).

3. Willard M. Wallace, *Sir Walter Raleigh* (Princeton, 1959), p. 158.

4. For Eden's working methods see Elizabeth Baer, 'Richard Eden's Copy of the 1533 *Decades* of Peter Martyr', in *Essays Honoring Lawrence C*

Wroth, ed. Frederick R. Goff *et al.* (Portland, Maine, 1951), pp. 3–14. The editions of his works referred to are *A treatyse of the newe India – after the description of Sebastian Münster in his book of universall Cosmographie* (London, 1553); *The Decades of the newe worlde or west India, . . . translated into Englyssche by Rycharde Eden* (London, 1555); *De novo orbe, or the historie of the West Indies* (London, 1612), which was the first complete English translation of all eight decades; and *The Famous Historie Of The Indies . . . comprised into sundry Decades* (London, 1628). Peter Martyr was Pietro Martire d'Anghiera (1457–1526).

5. Richard Haklyut (compiler), *Divers voyages touching the discoverie of America, and the Ilands adiacent unto the same, made first of all by our Englishmen, and afterward by the Frenchmen and Britons* (London, 1582).

6. Because of its confidential nature, the *editio princeps* is *A discourse on western planting, written in the year 1584, by Richard Hakluyt. With a preface and an introduction by Leonard Woods*, ed. Charles Deane (Maine Historical Society, Cambridge, 1877). For the background to the writing of the memorandum see *The Hakluyt Handbook*, ed. D.B. Quinn (The Hakluyt Society, 2nd series no. 144, London, 1974), vol. I, pp. 284–6.

7. The frontispiece to John Dee's *Pety Navy Royall* (London, 1577), is reproduced in E.G.R. Taylor, *Late Tudor and Early Stuart Geography 1583–1650* (London, 1934), Plate II. For Dee see Gwy A. Williams, *Madoc: The Making of a Myth* (London, 1979), and Peter G. French, *John Dee: The World of an Elizabethan Magus* (London, 1972).

8. D.B. Quinn, *Set Fair for Roanoke: Voyages and Colonies, 1584–1606* (Chapel Hill and London, 1984) is now the definitive study of the Roanoke ventures.

9. K.R. Andrews, *Elizabethan Privateering* (Cambridge, 1964); Clive Senior, *A Nation of Pirates: English Piracy in its Heyday* (London, 1976).

10. Michael Edwardes, *Ralph Fitch, Elizabethan in the Indies* (London, 1972).

11. *The Voyages of Sir James Lancaster, Kt., To The East Indies*, ed. Clemens R. Markham (London, The Hakluyt Society, vol. LVI, 1877).

12. Ruth A. MacIntyre, *Debts Hopeful and Desperate: Financing the Plymouth Colony* (Plimoth Plantation, 1963).

13. Bernard Bailyn, *The New England Merchants in the Seventeenth Century* (New York, 1964).

14. Thad W. Tate and David L. Ammerman (eds), *The Chesapeake in the Seventeenth Century: Essays on Anglo-American Society and Politics* (New York, 1979).

15. William Foster (ed.), *The Embassy of Sir Thomas Roe To The Court of The Great Mogul, 1615–1619* (London, The Hakluyt Society, 2nd series, vols. I and II, 1899), vol. II, p. 344.

16. I. Bruce Watson, 'Fortifications and the "Idea" of Force in Early English

East India Company Relations with India', *Past and Present* 88 (1980), pp. 70–87.

17. Maurice Ashley, *Financial and Commercial Policy under the Cromwellian Protectorate* (2nd edn, London, 1962), pp. 24–5, 132–8, and 161–9.

18. David Ogg, *England in the Reign of Charles II* (2nd edn, one vol. paperback reprint, Oxford, 1972), pp. 386–8.

19. Arthur Bryant, *Samuel Pepys: The Years of Peril* (Reprint Soc. edn, London, 1952), ch. VI, 'The Thirty New Ships'.

20. Stephen Saunders Webb, *The Governors-General: The English Army and the Definition of the Empire, 1569–1681* (Chapel Hill, 1979), Part III.

21. Philip S. Haffenden, 'The Crown and the Colonial Charters, 1675–1688', parts I and II, *The William and Mary Quarterly*, XV (1958), pp. 297–311, and 452–66.

22. H.F. Dickinson, *Liberty and Property: Political Ideology in Eighteenth-Century Britain* (London, 1977), and J.P. Kenyon, *Revolution Principles: The Politics of Party 1687–1720* (Cambridge, 1977).

23. David S. Lovejoy, *The Glorious Revolution in America* (New York, 1974), and Bernard Bailyn, *The Ideological Origins of the American Revolution* (Cambridge, Mass., paperback edn, 1976).

24. 'The Botching Taylor butting his cloth to cover a button' is a 1779 cartoon numbered 5573 in M.D. George, *Catalogue of Political and Personal Satires Preserved in the Department of Prints and Drawings in the British Museum*, vol. V, 1771–83 (London, 1935). For help with the cartoon material I am deeply indebted to the staff of the John Carter Brown Library, Providence, Rhode Island, and especially the Curator of Maps.

25. 'By His Majesty's Royal Letters etc.', ibid., no. 5580, shows Liberty flying up the road to America.

26. 'The Tea-Tax Tempest, Or the Anglo-American Revolution', ibid., no. 5490, is a fine image of an empire blowing up around a teapot. There is a reduced version with a balloon coming out of Father Time's mouth which is British Museum cartoon 6190. The John Carter Brown Library has a contemporary version which is tinted garishly but effectively.

12. Britain under Westminster *L.M. Cullen*

1. D.B. Quinn and A.N. Ryan, *England's Sea Empire, 1550–1642* (London, 1983).

2. H. Fenwick, *The Auld Alliance* (Kineton, 1971).

3. *A New History of Ireland*, vol. III, *Early Modern Ireland 1534–1691* (Oxford, 1976), ed. T.W. Moody, F.X. Martin and F.J. Byrne, pp. 103–4, 107–8, 132–5.

4. D.B. Quinn, *The Elizabethans and the Irish* (Ithaca, New York, 1966).

5. *Ulster and Other Irish Maps, c. 1600*, ed. G.A. Hayes-McCoy (Dublin, 1964).

6. *Négociations de M. Le Comte d'Avaux en Irlande* (Dublin, 1934), ed. J. Hogan, provides a very clear picture of the organisation and management of the French troops in Ireland.

7. There were of course a number of reasons for the Union. See P.W.J. Riley, *The Union of England and Scotland* (Edinburgh, 1978), p. 8.

8. B. Lenman, *The Jacobite Risings in Britain 1689–1746* (Edinburgh, 1980).

9. J.B. Salmond, *Wade in Scotland* (Edinburgh and London, 1938).

10. L.M. Cullen, 'Merchant Communities Overseas, the Navigation Acts and Irish and Scottish Responses', in L.M. Cullen and T.C. Smout (eds), *Comparative Aspects of Scottish and Irish Economic and Social History 1600–1900* (Edinburgh, 1977), pp. 165–7.

11. J.M. Price, *France and the Chesapeake,* 2 vols (Ann Arbor, 1973).

12. B. Behrens, 'Nobles, Privileges and Taxes in France at the End of the Ancien Regime', *Economic History Review,* 2nd series (April, 1963), p. 463 and 463n.

13. R.S. Neale, *Bath 1680–1850: a Social History* (London, 1981).

14. E.A. Wrigley and R.S. Schofield, *The Population of England, 1541–1871* (London, 1981), pp. 210, 224.

15. On the army, see S.H.F. Johnson, 'The Irish Establishment', *Irish Sword,* vol. I (1949–50), pp. 33–6; F.G. James, *Ireland in the Empire 1688–1770* (Harvard, 1973), pp. 175–81; John Childs, *The Army of Charles II* (London, 1976), pp. 196–209; H.C.B. Rogers, *The British Army of the Eighteenth Century* (London, 1976).

16. In 1719 the Irish and British army establishments were equal, each having 12,000 men. Previously the peacetime establishment in Ireland had been larger; from 1720 the peacetime establishments were: Ireland, 12,000; Britain, 18,000.

17. G. Donaldson, *The Scots Overseas* (London, 1966), pp. 61–5.

18. R.B. McDowell, 'Ireland in the Eighteenth-Century British Empire', in *Historical Studies,* ed. J.G. Barry, vol. IX (Belfast, 1974), pp. 61–2.

19. The best account of Dublin remains M.J. Craig, *Dublin 1660–1860: a Social and Architectural History* (London, 1952).

20. S. Johnson, *Journey to the Western Isles of Scotland and Boswell's Journal of a Tour of the Hebrides* (Oxford, 1924), p. 422.

21. Public Record Office of Northern Ireland, letters of Baron Willes, *c.* 1760 (microfilm).

Notes
on Contributors

ELIZABETH COOK worked for her doctorate at the Earburg Institute, University of London. She works as a freelance writer and speaker and is currently preparing an edition of Keats.

LOUIS CULLEN is a Fellow of Trinity College, Dublin, Professor of Modern Irish History, and member of the Royal Irish Academy. He is a graduate of University College, Galway, and completed his PhD studies at the London School of Economics. He is a specialist of the eighteenth century, and his current interests lie mainly in comparative history, and in the overlap between economic, social and political factors. His publications include *Life in Ireland* (1968), *Anglo-Irish Trade, 1660–1800* (1968), *An Economic History of Ireland since 1660* (1972), *The Emergence of Modern Ireland, 1600–1900* (1981) and *Princes and Pirates: the Dublin Chamber of Commerce, 1783–1983* (1983). He is joint editor of several volumes on comparative themes in French, Irish and Scottish history.

MARK GOLDIE is a Fellow and Lecturer in History at Churchill College, Cambridge. He was an undergraduate at Sussex University, before moving to Cambridge, where he was awarded his PhD in 1978. He has published several articles on the politics, political theory and religious history of later Stuart England. He has a book, *The Tory Ideology: Politics, Religion, and Ideas in Restoration England*, forthcoming.

CHRISTOPHER HAIGH is tutor in Modern History at Christ Church, and Lecturer in Modern History at Oxford University. He has written two books on the Reformation in the north-west of England, and a number of articles which have sought to reinterpret the English Reformation and its aftermath. He is the editor of *The Reign of Elizabeth I* (1984) and of *The Cambridge Historical Encyclopedia of Great Britain and Ireland* (1985). He is now writing books on the Reformation in England and on the Church of England and its people between 1559 and 1642.

RONALD HUTTON has taken degrees at Cambridge and Oxford and was a Fellow of Magdalen College, Oxford, before being appointed to his present post in the Department of History at Bristol University. He has written books on the Civil War and the Restoration period, and is at present working upon two more, concerning Charles II and popular festivals.

BRUCE LENMAN was educated at St John's College, Cambridge, and is now a Reader in Modern History at the University of St Andrews. His research interests centre on the history of Britain during the seventeenth and eighteenth centuries. His books include *An Economic History of Scotland* (1977), *The Jacobite Risings in Britain* (1980) and *Integration, Enlightenment and Industrialisation: Scotland 1746–1832* (1982).

KEVIN SHARPE is lecturer in History at Southampton University. A graduate of Oxford and former Fellow of Oriel College, he has been a Visiting Fellow of the Institute for Advanced Study, Princeton, and the Huntington Library. Currently, he is Visiting Professor at Stamford University Humanities Centre. He is the editor of *Faction and Parliament* (1978) and of *Politics of Discourse* (forthcoming), and the author of *Sir Robert Cotton: History and Politics in Early Modern England* (1979) and *Criticism and Compliment: The Politics of Literature in the England of Charles I* (forthcoming). He is completing a study of the Personal Rule of Charles I.

LESLEY M. SMITH, the editor, studied history at the University of St Andrews and Brasenose College, Oxford. She now works as a researcher for London Weekend Television. She has edited (with Geoffrey Parker) *The General Crisis of the Seventeenth Century* (1978) and also the first two books in the *Making of Britain* series: *The Dark Ages* (1984) and *The Middle Ages* (1985).

WILLIAM SPECK was educated at Bradford Grammar School and The Queen's College, Oxford. Since graduating from Oxford University where he obtained his DPhil, he has taught at the Universities of Exeter, Newcastle-upon-Tyne and Hull. Currently he is Professor of Modern History at the University of Leeds. His publications are primarily about various aspects of eighteenth century English history and include a textbook, *Stability and Strife: England 1714–1760*. He is presently engaged in a study of the Glorious Revolution of 1688.

MARGARET SPUFFORD was a research scholar of the Department of English Local History at Leicester from 1960–3, where she collected the material which lay behind her *Contrasting Communities*, published in 1974 with the support of a research fellowship from Lucy Cavendish College, Cambridge. In 1974, she became an Honorary Lecturer at the University of Keele and worked on cheap print and its readership for *Small Books and Pleasant Histories*. From 1978–80, the Social Science Research Council provided her with a Senior Research Fellowship, held at Keele, to work on pedlars and their goods. In 1981, she was elected a Fellow of Newnham College, Cambridge, and is now writing a seventeenth-century social history.

DAVID STARKEY teaches history at the London School of Economics. His research interests centre on the Tudor court, but also range widely through sixteenth-century administration, culture and politics. He has written several articles and a book, *The Reign of Henry VIII: Politics and Personalities* (1985). He is co-editor, with Christopher Coleman, of *Revolution Reassessed* (1985); presenter and deviser of the Channel Four series *This Land of England*, and joint author, with David Souden, of the accompanying book.

JENNY WORMALD was a Lecturer in Scottish History in the University of Glasgow, and is now Fellow of St Hilda's College, Oxford. She edited and contributed to *Scottish Society in the Fifteenth Century* (1977) and was general editor of the *New History of Scotland*, and author of vol. 4, *Court, Kirk and Community: Scotland 1470–1625* (1981). She has recently published *Lords and Men in Scotland: Bonds of Manrent, 1442–1603* (1985). Her major research interest has been the monarchy and nobility of late-medieval and early-modern Scotland. She is now researching a book on James VI and I.

KEITH WRIGHTSON was born in County Durham in 1948. He was educated at Dame Allen's School, Newcastle-upon-Tyne and at Fitzwilliam College, Cambridge. He graduated in 1970 and began research on English social history under the supervision of Peter Laslett. He has been Research Fellow at Fitzwilliam College, Cambridge (1972–5), Lecturer in Modern History at the University of St Andrews (1975–84), and a Canadian Commonwealth Fellow. At present he is a University Lecturer in History at Cambridge and a Fellow of Jesus College.

Index